MONSIGNOR EMILE GUERRY
ARCHBISHOP OF CAMBRAI

The Social Teaching
of the Church

*"The Church is the standard-bearer of
a way of life which is ever up-to-date...
We reaffirm strongly that this social
doctrine is an integral part of the
Christian conception of life"*
(John XXIII, 'Mater et Magistra')

ST PAUL PUBLICATIONS
LONDON — NEW YORK — BOMBAY

This translation of La Doctrine Sociale de l'Eglise
(Bonne Press, Paris) was made by
MIRIAM HEDERMAN

NIHIL OBSTAT : E. HARDWICK, *Censor deputatus*

IMPRIMATUR : + CAROLUS GRANT, *Ep. Alind., Vic. Gen.*
Northantoniae, die 19a *iunii* 1961

Made and printed in the United Kingdom
by the Society of St. Paul, Langley, Bucks.

THE SOCIAL TEACHING OF THE CHURCH

A

FOREWORD

This splendid exposition of Catholic social teaching should be read and re-read by all Catholics and by all others who are seriously interested in modern social thought. It appears at a remarkably appropriate moment. The tremendous impact of the new Encyclical of Pope John XXIII should be causing great numbers of Catholics and non-Catholics to inquire afresh into the basic traditions of Catholic social principles. These could not be better presented than in the ensuing text. We are told here that the social teaching of the Church is extracted from Revelation and the natural law which it applies to the social problems of our time. This means in terms of modern academic disciplines a drawing together of theology, philosophy and the social sciences. Many of the divisions and much of the incoherence of secular thinking today in Britain derives from a compartmentalism which shuts off these different approaches to truth in separate pigeon holes, and Catholics themselves are seldom free from blame in this respect. Few of us have a truly integrated view of man in his relation to society. Few of us when involved in practical politics or social reform can claim to remain in constant touch with fundamental realities.

One rises from this book with a new appreciation of the building of thought and experience on each other and above all, with a fresh glimpse of how a Catholic inspiration could help us to visualise a better world and strengthen us in our efforts to achieve it.

Lord Longford

CONTENTS

Introduction

THE IMPORTANCE OF THE SOCIAL TEACHING
OF THE CHURCH

19

I

WHAT IS THE SOCIAL TEACHING OF THE CHURCH?

The Sources   21
The Author   24
The Object and Content   26
The Purpose   27

II

WHY HAS THE CHURCH A SOCIAL DOCTRINE?

1) Educator of man's conscience   29
2) Guardian of the Moral Law   32
3) The Mystical Body of Christ   38

III

THE OBJECTIONS

1) The Church's social teaching is an anachronism ...   40
2) Christian civilisation   40
3) Secularism : The States' fear of the Church's
   encroachment   42
4) The secularism of the State   43
5) The social teaching of the Church is addressed
   only to Christians   45
6) The two-fold source of the Church's social teaching ...   46
7) The social teaching of the Church is too rigid
   in its principles and too vague in their application ...   47
8) The very name "Social Doctrine"   49

CLOSE OF INTRODUCTION

51

PART I

A CONCEPT OF MAN

First Principle :

THE DIGNITY OF THE HUMAN PERSON

The fundamental basis of this dignity   55
The application of the principle   58

Second Principle :

FUNDAMENTAL EQUALITY OF MEN

I. The principle   61
II. The results and practical consequences of this
    principle   62
III. Natural and social inequalities contrasted with
     the principle of the equality of men   64

Third Principle :

THE INALIENABLE RIGHTS OF MAN, WHO IS THE SUBJECT AND NOT THE OBJECT OF THESE RIGHTS

I. *The principle: Man is a subject and not a mere object*   69
   Applications :
   — in the social relations between employers
    and workers   70
   — in dealing with the national economy   70
   — before the law   70
II. *The fundamental rights of man*   71
   The fundamental rights of the human person   71
   First right : right to material possessions   72
   Principles of the right of ownership   73
   1) The resources of creation are destined for all
     and the goods of the earth are meant to be
     shared   73
   Application on the international plane and with-
   in a single nation   74
   2) The distinction between the right of ownership
     and use   76

Practical applications :

    First case : in the normal way in the ordinary
    course of life 77

    Second case : in extreme necessity 79

3) The vital function of private ownership must
    be respected and protected in its personal and
    social role—its legality 79

4) The present system of ownership is not un-
    changeable 80

Conclusions 80

Second right : the right to work 82

First characteristic of work : it is *personal* 82

Applications :

— dignity of work 83

— conditions of work 83

— the duty of the State 84

Second characteristic of work : it is *necessary* 84

Principle 84

Practical applications :

1) for the remuneration of work 84

    — the living wage 85

    — the family wage 86

2) organisation of work 88

    — fight against unemployment 87

Third characteristic of work : it is *social* 87

    The high moral value of work 88

CONCLUSION TO PART ONE

The concept of man as underlined in the teachings
of Pope Pius XII 89

Intense humanity 89

Its dynamic realism 89

Defence of man against the perils that menace him 90

Concept of man as he is 91

PART II

THE CHRISTIAN CONCEPT
OF THE SOCIAL ECONOMY

The Christian concept of the social economy can be recognised by the following characteristics :

First Characteristic

A HUMAN ECONOMY

in as much as

1) it should be *at the service of man*
   The primacy of man   95
2) it should take into consideration *human nature
   and the whole man*   96
3) it should adjust itself *to man's fundamental needs* ...   97
4) it should aim *at man's improvement*
   An economy of human progress, of material prosperity for the whole population   99
5) it should make its benefits *available to all men* 101
6) it should fit *man* and be *made to human scale*   101
   The relevance of a human economy   103

Second Characteristic

AN ECONOMY FOR THE COMMON GOOD

I. What is the common good?
   Definition of Pope Pius XII   104
II. What are the essential components of the common good?   106
   1) public and external order   106
   2) material prosperity for the whole population   107
   3) higher values of the intellectual, spiritual,
      moral and religious order   108
III. The greatness and importance of the common
   good   109
IV. The service of the common good   111
   The mission of the State   111
Conclusion : the relevance and influence of this chapter of the Church's social teaching   113

Third Characteristic

AN ORGANIC ECONOMY

I. In the sense that is should help to give society
the unity of an organism 115
Objection : class warfare 116
II. In the sense that it is based on *vocational organi-sation* in all branches of production 118
The programme of the Popes 119
1) The Trade Unions 120
2) The Vocational Organisation 120
Its advantages 122
3) The legal structure of economic and social life organised on a professional basis 122
Distinction between private and public rights ... 123
Planning : the State's mission 124
Dangers of over-rigid planning and an in-human technocracy 125
Nationalisation 128
Structural reforms of enterprise 129
Conclusion : The present position of the problem of vocational organisation 131

Fourth Characteristic

A DYNAMIC ECONOMY INSPIRED BY SOCIAL JUSTICE AND CHARITY

I. *Social Justice* 134
1) Its objective : the various forms of justice 134
2) The basis of social justice 136
3) The requirements of social justice 137
4) The scope of social justice 138
II. *Social Charity* 139
Charity which concerns itself with the common good : new motives, a new objective, a new principle 140
A dynamic aspect of the virtues of social justice and social charity 140

Fifth Characteristic

AN ECONOMY SUBORDINATE TO THE MORAL LAW

Distinction, not separation between economy and the
moral law   141

I. *Judgement on different economies not in accord
with the moral law*   124

   1) Economic Liberalism   142

   — Liberal Capitalism — Teachings of the Popes   144

   2) Communism   146

   — Why has the Church condemned it?   146

   — Experience of Communism in Soviet Russia in relation to the moral law   147

II. *Reforms in practice*   151

Revolution, reform or transformation?   151

Teaching of the Church   151

The social doctrine of the Church aims at a complete transformation of society in its entire structure   152

CONCLUSION

The fundamental principles of the social teaching of
the Church   155

The extent of the social teaching - the great work of
rebuilding a new world towards which the Church
invites the co-operation of men of action of all walks
of life   159

The authority of Papal Documents   160

Attitude of the faithful to the teaching of the Ordinary Magisterium   162

   1) Respect   162

   2) Study of the *degree* of authority exercised by
each particular document   162

   3) Acceptance and obedience...   164

Bibliography   169

Index   165

Mother and Teacher   171

INTRODUCTION

THE IMPORTANCE OF THE SOCIAL TEACHING
OF THE CHURCH :

ITS BINDING FORCE

How many Catholics believe, in all good faith, that their Church's social teaching is a matter of choice, a sort of optional doctrine? This serious mistake is undoubtedly responsible for the ignorance, neglect and abandonment of the social doctrine of the Church in France and elsewhere for the past ten years.

It is important to make quite clear, at the very outset, that a Catholic worthy of the name, is obliged to follow the social teaching of his Church. The Hierarchy is explicit on the point. Pope Pius XII, speaking of the social doctrine of the Church, in 1945, declared : *"It is binding: no-one can ignore it without danger to Faith and Morals"* [1] In 1947 the Holy Father vigorously re-affirmed that this social teaching of the Church shows us the way to follow and that nothing, "no fear of loss of worldly goods or benefits, no fear of seeming opposed to modern civilisation nor of appearing unpatriotic or lacking in social consciousness, can excuse true Christians for deviating, even by a single step from this path". [2]

In 1952, the Pope, speaking to Austrian Catholics and, through them, to *"all the faithful"*, exhorted them "to follow faithfully the clear line of Catholic Social Doctrine ... without deviating to right or left. A deviation of only a few degrees can seem unimportant in the beginning. In the long run this deviation will lead to a dangerous separation from the right path". [3]

In France "The Pastoral Directory in Social Matters for the Use of the Clergy" adopted by the Plenary Assembly of the Hierarchy, 27th April, 1954, lays down in Article 24, "the priest should never deviate from the social teaching of the Church".

(1) Pope Pius XII, Allocution to the Congress of Italian Catholic Action, 29th April, 1945.
(2) Different features, consciously or not, can be invoked: some by industrialists others by militant workers or intellectuals.
(3) Pope Pius XII, Radio Message to Austrian Catholics, 14th Sept. 1952.

Furthermore, Article 76 recalls the passage in the Exhortation, *Menti nostrae* in which Pope Pius XII declares that "the damage caused by the two economic systems (capitalism and communism) should convince everyone, and priests in particular, that they should *adhere and remain faithful to the social teaching of the Church*".

Finally, the second Plenary Assembly of the Hierarchy (April 1954) held, in its doctrinal declaration, that "*one of the gravest failings of the present day is the underestimation or ignorance of the social teaching of the Church*".

Such warnings from Pope and bishops impose a duty in conscience to know, study and propagate the social teaching of the Church. It is therefore of the greatest importance that we should know exactly what this teaching is. Unfortunately, there are misunderstandings and confusions on this point which must be cleared up for they are responsible, in great measure, for the lamentable attitude of many Christians.

I.

WHAT IS THE SOCIAL TEACHING OF THE CHURCH ?

The Social Teaching of the Church is an embodiment of concepts, (composed of truths, principles and values) which the living Magisterium extracts from Revelation and the natural law and adapts and applies to the social problems of our times in order to help, as the Church should, peoples and governments to organise a more human society in accordance with God's plan for the world.

This definition of the social teaching of the Church sets out its sources, author, content, object and purpose.

I.   The Sources :

The concepts which make up the social teaching of the Church are drawn *"from Revelation and the natural law"* by the living Magisterium.

1.   *The natural law :* is that inscribed by the Creator in man's very being, in his animal and rational nature, as understood by his intelligence. It is the expression in us of what our reason demands; it informs our conscience of what we should do to act in accordance with our rational nature, so that we may not go against all that is good and noble in man. It tells us to "do good and avoid evil"; good being what is in accordance with our rational nature — evil being what destroys its true development.

Chapter One will show the application which the Popes have made of the natural law to *the true concept of man* in order to establish his fundamental rights and duties, his dignity and legitimate freedom.

In the second chapter we shall see how Pope Pius XII in particular, based his conception of the social economy on the natural law, placing man in the scope of the science of social economics. For the Pope this science is not only the study of physical and mechanical phenomena but also of *human acts* — the acts of free men who ought to co-operate in the building of a social order in conformity with the order made known by God in the natural law and Revelation. Certain economists erred by failing to appreciate the true nature of man and fell into a pitfall on this proposition.

"The natural law is the foundation on which rests the social teaching of the Church", declared Pope Pius XII. [4]

2. *Revelation.* Human reason has the power to discover and understand, through its own resources, the truths of the natural law and, from these truths, to come to a true knowledge of a personal God. Nevertheless, because of the results of original sin and the passions which always threaten to cloud the intelligence and prevent man from seeing clearly and from judging correctly and without self-deception, the Vatican Council defined that, even for the truths of reason, Revelation, as well as the authentic teaching of the Church, is morally necessary in the present state of the human race. Revelation confirms the natural law. It surpasses, expands, and deepens it.

There is a double Revelation : that of the Old and the New Testament.

a) *Revelation of the Old Testament.* As well as the cultural and judicial laws, the Old Testament contains a *moral law* which is an expression of the natural law. The Decalogue sets out duties to God, rights and duties concerning the human person, the family, the neighbour. Except for the Third Commandment, which contains a positive divine command to reserve the Lord's Day for divine worship, [5] the other commandments do not go beyond the

---

(4) Allocution to the members of the Congress of humanistic studies, 25th September, 1952.

(5) The 3rd Commandment defines, in a concrete manner, the precept of the natural law to consecrate time to the Lord.

resources of human reason. They are, therefore, binding as an expression of the natural law but their authority is reinforced by the fact that they are a positive manifestation of the Divine will and because they are part of the great and free gift of God's Covenant.

On the social plane, a most important place must be accorded to the Prophets who denounced injustice, proclaimed the rights of the poor and lowly and preached social and religious justice.

b) *Revelation of the New Testament.* Jesus Christ Himself said that He did not come to abolish the Old Law but to perfect it, particularly by the New Commandment : "Love one another as I have loved you". [6] The New Law is that of charity which invests all virtues, particularly justice, with the grace of the Holy Spirit. The Gospels contain a complete teaching on riches and poverty, the use of the fruits of the earth and the establishment of a human community in which all men partake of the world's goods, destined by God to be thus shared.

But the Double Revelation, as consistently unfolded through the ages, consists more in God's great design for the salvation of mankind than in particular precepts on one virtue or another.

God calls man to share in the free gift of His Divine Life — man refuses the gift and falls into sin — God decides, in His infinite mercy, to save him. He stirs up His chosen people, moulds them and guides them by His Word. He speaks through His patriarchs and prophets who foretell the Messiah, Redeemer of His people. He speaks finally through His Son, Whom He sends into the world to save all men. Jesus Christ, the Incarnate Word, redeems humanity by His message of truth, His life, death and resurrection. He founds the Church which He makes His social Body, animated by His Spirit. As Head of this Body He leads His people through mankind's social life and history so that they may bring together all men in unity and thus form the Whole Christ by the growth

---

(6) The Revelation of the New Testament takes up the precept of charity, extending it to all men and all nations and teaching that it is realised in Christ as the model and source of this love.

of this Body in charity.   This is the plan for salvation the Church has reflected in its tradition and written into its dogma : Jesus Christ, the Son of God, is Mediator between God and men, the only Saviour; and the Church is messenger of the Truth, guardian of the moral law, the means of salvation, teacher of mankind through its different activities here on earth.

The Fathers of the Church applied this far-reaching plan of salvation to the social problems of their time in a very daring and vigorous moral doctrine on the use of wealth and the distribution of the fruits of the earth. It is the same Divine plan for mankind which to-day inspires the Magisterium's intervention in the economic and social field. It is understood that the Church's social teaching derives its meaning from the wide perspective of God's plan for salvation. It is obvious, in reason and faith, that it must bind the Church's children.

2. *The Author (the efficient cause).*

It is necessary to make a most important clarification here to dispel many misunderstandings and ambiguities about the social teaching of the Church. Many active Christians still refuse to subscribe to the social teaching of the Church because certain schools of thought have quoted this teaching to justify positions or courses with which they did not agree.

Pope Pius XII has himself made a clear distinction in this debate :

"This Institution (the Gregorium University) has undertaken the teaching of the social doctrine of the Church whose principle points are contained in the documents of the Holy See, that is to say, in the Encyclicals, the Allocutions and the Papal Letters. On this subject different social schools have appeared which have explained the pontifical documents and have developed and classified them. We think that they were right in so doing. But it was impossible to avoid that, in the application of principles and conclusions, these same schools should not move apart and fairly often differ among themselves. Also in this context, what we said earlier about the teaching of the Catholic faith and theological schools must be remembered and care must be taken not to confuse the authentic doctrine of the Church with the different positions taken by each school; the two aspects should be always distinguished with great care". [7]

Thus, two aspects should be carefully separated : on the one hand, the authentic social doctrine of the Church; on the other, the application of principles and conclusions in which one can discern different theologians, sociologists, schools and movements.

The work, research and positions of these Christian economists and these schools do not constitute the social teaching of the Church herself. *Before* the intervention of the Magisterium they could play a very important part in preparing and making available vital documentation and information. *After* the publication of the pontifical document they seek to comment on its teaching and explain it. But neither the preliminary work nor the studies, no matter how great their intrinsic value, nor how authoritative their propounders, form the official social teaching of the Church.

The Pope's comparison is very enlightening : a clear distinction must be made between the teaching of the Catholic faith by the Magisterium on the one hand and, on the other hand, the different theological schools which do not in themselves as systems constitute an entry into the Church nor, more particularly, the only entry. The Church alone is the gateway to salvation and, under the protection and guidance of the Holy Spirit, the source of all truth. The living Magisterium is the proximate and universal measure of the true meaning of the social teaching of the Church as it is of every other branch of doctrine. [8]

---

(7) Pope Pius XII, Discourse for the IVth Centenary of the Gregorian University in Rome, 17th October, 1953. (Documentation Catholique, 7th February, 1954.)

(8) As we shall see later, Christians must apply themselves, under their own responsibility, to political, economic and social analyses and draw their conclusions with a view to action. **The social teaching of the Church is not a ready-made programme which has only to be applied. Christians still have to work out a programme of action,** which, while it refers to this doctrine will imply ideas and applications which are the complete responsibilities of the laity.

3. *The object and content of the Church's social teaching:*

We have defined the social teaching of the Church as "an ensemble of concepts, made up of truths, principles and values".
— the truths are what one has to believe and know (moral and religious truths);
— the principles are what one has to do, put into practice (code of moral behaviour);
— the values are what one has to respect, defend and cherish (fundamental human rights).

These are concepts drawn from the natural law and Revelation. The living Magisterium adapts and applies them to the social problems which arise in the changing circumstances of economic and social life.

Revelation brought a Christian concept of man, his origin, nature, dignity and destiny — a Christian concept of the world, of history, of social life and of the human community — a Christian concept of work, of the realities of life, of love, of the family, etc. The social teaching of the Church is the application of these Christian concepts to the review of present socio-economic structures and to the building of a more truly human, social and economic order.

Whenever the Magisterium intervenes through its social teaching it does so in the name of truth and of principles which are *sub specie aeternitatis* and in *the light of the divine law,* [9]*irrespective of whether it is a question of faith or morals,* that is, of the conduct of the *social* man and of his way of life. If the Church intervenes it does so to protect and safeguard those supreme values [10] of the dignity of man and the eternal salvation of souls.

But the action of the Church as guardian of the deposit of faith and the moral law can appear under different guises. Some-

(9) Pope Pius XII, Radio Message to the world, 24th December, 1951.
(10) P.P.XII "The Church will fight with all her forces **where the supreme values are at stake**: the dignity of man and the eternal salvation of souls". Message to Austrian Catholics, 14th September, 1952.

times she *teaches* these principles and ideas directly; sometimes she *defends* and protects these values by her judgements on erroneous theories (liberalism, communism, nazism) or the economic structures which threaten them, (technocracy, state totalitarianism); other times again she proposes the concrete *application* of these principles (vocational organisations) and herself furthers their application as circumstances and place require. It is important to study the documents very carefully in order to distinguish in them absolute truths, and directives, and their pastoral application as made by the Church — the latter requiring careful judgement.

4. *The Purpose*

The *essential object* of the Church's social teaching is the advancement of the *Kingdom of God* through human relations and temporal realities for the salvation of men. In this way she wishes to fulfil her spiritual mission to unite all men in God and among themselves. This of course causes her to condemn whatever operates against this end and to support whatever furthers it. She cannot remain indifferent as to whether or not men and nations are on good terms with each other. Essentially evangelical, the Church becomes, in addition, a civilising influence.

But the Church also pursues a proximate objective. She cannot, by herself, build an earthly city nor organise a temporal society. She leaves this to governments and nations. But "Guardian, by the will and order of Christ of the natural and supernatural order [11] educator of mankind, Mother who cannot remain deaf to the anguished cries which her children of all classes of mankind" [12] send up to her, the Church wants to help men to build a more human, more just, more brotherly society which will be more in accordance with God's plan for man and the human community. Our definition adds that this intervention is *"as the Church should"* that is, in the course of her particular mission and by an educational method which will be described later[13]. In purely temporal

(11) P.P. XII, Radio Message to the World, 24th December, 1942.
(12) Radio Message, Christmas, 1942.

affairs the Church does not take the place of the State nor of the civil sphere of authority in the building and running of the earthly City. She leaves them their creative work, just as God committed creation to man so that he could fulfil it by his work, his intelligence and his efforts. She never ceases to proclaim that she does not attempt to *"lay down rules for the purely technical aspects of the social organisation"*. [14] But she shows the road to be followed. She gives all the heritage and values of the Christian life so that each one can draw on them according to his own particular genius and his special needs in order *"to set up a society worthy of man, raise it to a spiritual level and provide true well-being"*. [15]

CONCLUSION

In his Christmas message of 1955, Pope Pius XII declared that there are *"false or restricted visions of the world and of life accepted by modern men"* and these prevent men from going to the heart of things and from recognising the foundation which gives meaning and harmony to human actions.

The Pope, on the contrary, *gave a wide and true vision* in his messages to the faithful and to the entire world. *The Social Teaching of the Church is the projection into the social and economic order of this great vision of the world and of life: it affirms "the absolute order of beings and ends"*[16] *according to reason and the Christian faith.*

(13) See reply to Objection number three.

(14) P.P. XII, Radio Message, 1st June, 1941.

(15) P.P. XII, Radio Message, 24th December, 1940: "Guardian and mistress of the principles of faith and morals, her only interest and desire is to give all nations, without exception, with her education and religious methods, the clear source of the heritage and values of the Christian life, so that each nation, according to its particular characteristics, makes use of the doctrines and ethico-religious features of Christianity in order to establish a worthily human society, which will be highly spiritual and a source of true well-being".

(16) P.P. XII, Radio Message, 24th December, 1944.

II.

WHY HAS THE CHURCH A SOCIAL DOCTRINE ?

There are three primary reasons why the Church should have and teach a social doctrine. Each is closely bound up with the Church's mission.

Reason One : As *educator of man's conscience* the Church should lead *each human being* to his supernatural destiny through the realities of this life.

Reason Two : As *guardian of the moral law* the Church has the right and duty to denounce all attacks by *economic and social institutions* against the moral law.

Reason Three : As the *Mystical Body* the Church has the mission of uniting all men in the unity of the love of Christ.

First Reason : As the educator of man's conscience the Church should lead human beings to their supernatural destiny through the realities of this life.

It is in everyday things, in family life and in working, economic and social affairs that men find, or lose, their eternal salvation. How? By *acting in accordance* with the moral law as laid down in the Commandments of God and in the Gospels.

In more concrete terms, it is in the conscientious fulfilment of their duties to God, the *duties of their state in life* (professional, political and social) that men are saved by the grace of Jesus Christ, that is, by practising, with the help of divine grace, the natural and supernatural *virtues* which their station in life requires.

The Mission of the Church

The Church, as teacher, helps men to recognise and fulfil their vocations and their destiny. She moulds their consciences to recognise the duties of their different spheres of human activity. She teaches them, in particular, that *the order of salvation pervades their whole economic and social life*. She reveals the true value of human endeavour in the divine plan. She reveals also the spiritual meaning of work, of human love, of married life, of art, technology, and all the activities of the human community. She shows men that civilisation needs redemption to rediscover its true meaning in accordance with God's plan. The world needs to be purified by Christ, the Redeemer, for it is no longer the world which God created. Sin has passed this way. And so the Church points out that civilisation can tend either to the progress of mankind, or to its destruction. The Church tries to make civilisation serve true progress and help man to achieve his final end. Her mission is to be of service and not to dominate.

The first aim of the social teaching of the Church is therefore to help Christians to fashion the world according to their faith. From this can be seen the light and strength of the faith for the building of the earthly City. The study of the obstacles to faith set up by conditions of life and work will be dealt with later.

Working Out of the Social Doctrine of the Church.

Certain developments of special importance have caused the Church, in turn, to develop her social doctrine so that she may fulfil her rôle of educator of man's conscience in this modern age.

First of all the *Industrial Revolution of the XIXth Century* caused considerable upheaval in the life of the individual, and of the family as well as in society generally and upset the traditional class relations. The Christian conscience was confronted with grave problems: how could the social injustice, which threw the mass of workers into undeserved misery, be righted? How could the crying inequality of the distribution of worldly goods be redressed? Had the workers the right to organise themselves to

protect their interests? Had the State the right to intervene with
social legislation to protect the weakest? How should the doctrines of liberalism and socialism be viewed?

To all these questions the Encyclical *Rerum Novarum* gave
the Church's answers. From then on a complete Catholic social
science grew from the teaching of the Popes who successively
replied to the problems of conscience posed by social evolution.

Furthermore, *"socialisation"* of human life developed rapidly
and the interdependence and solidarity between men, groups, professions and peoples quickly emerged. Ethics, which had become
excessively individualistic through historical circumstances, now
became *social ethics*. The Church has, by her teaching, faced up
to these new problems, and brought to light the virtues of social
justice and charity. It has sought to reconcile the claims of the
individual with the common good and showed how, according to
the plans of both nature and grace, man is, at the same time,
individual and communal.

Finally, a new phenomenon appeared with the progress of
civilisation : a *more acute consciousness* on the part of governments
and people, of the dignity of man and of his aspirations for a more
human life and for greater well-being. There was also recognition
for his rights and liberties and his participation in public life, as
well as for society's duties towards the underpriviledged and the po-
litically and economically weak. The duty to share the world's goods
more equitably among the underdeveloped peoples was acknow-
edged. Here again the social teaching of the Church guided each
one towards his destiny by means of those problems confronting
his conscience. The Popes, and more particularly Pope Pius XII,
taught a whole conception of man and his dignity, rights and
duties, as well as the proper use of freedom and its responsibilities.
The Head of the Church undertook the defence of the human
person against all the forces which threatened to come between it
and the fulfilment of its destiny. Could he have done more? The
problem posed by scientific and technical advances and their repercussions on the rapid evolution of the world is an enormous one.
It is all the more difficult because this evolution never ceases and
is even accelerating in certain sectors, outrunning the rhythm of

the analysis which economists, sociologists and politicians steadily and laboriously pursue.

Second Reason . As guardian of the moral law the Church cannot allow the social and economic order to violate the moral law when it should, in fact, serve to make it correspond to God's plan.

Since man should attain his destiny through upright living in the temporal order it is most important to realise that this temporal order (political, economic, social) does not itself constitute by its organisation, institutions, structures and spirit, *an obstacle* to the supreme destiny of the human person and of mankind. There are, however, societies and milieux where it is difficult, if not impossible, to remain faithful to the moral law and to live a Christian life.

For some time now religious sociology has established, by a detailed factual analysis, the deep, and often determining influence, wielded by social and economic conditions on the moral and social lives of men and their families. These include housing, transport, leisure, means of communication (press, cinema, radio, television). wages and working conditions, economic, political and social factors (like alcoholism and prostitution), natural groups, education and parental control (breaking up of family life).

As far back as 1931 Pope Pius XI said that the conditions of economic and social life are such that a very large number of people find the greatest difficulty in carrying out the work which, alone, is necessary for their eternal salvation [17].

The strong pronouncement made by Pope Pius XII on the disorder of the present economic society is also well known. "The Church cannot shut her eyes to the fact that the worker, in his effort to improve his condition, *comes up against a whole system which, far from being in accord with his nature, is in contradiction*

(17) P.P. XI, Quadragesimo Anno.

to the order of God, and His purpose for the fruits of the earth" [18].

Pius XII also affirmed the Church's right to have a social doctrine when he declared "incontestable ... the Church's competence in that sector of the social order which comes in contact with the moral law, to judge *if the basis of a given social organisation is in conformity with the 'immutable order proclaimed by God in the natural law and in Revelation'* " [19].

Because a materialistic age and a false philosophy have misunderstood the true meaning of man and of his nature — because the rights of workers have been violated by an excess of free enterprise and an unbridled desire for profit — because the economic regime has left innumerable workers' families without hope of justice, charity or humanity, in an "undeserved misery" according to Leo XIII, because the national and international political order has been falsified, the Church has worked out her social doctrine.

She intervenes as guardian of the moral law. But she also acts under the title of Mother. As Mother she loves her children and cannot accept any situation which would harm them.

As Pope Pius XII said : "How could the Church, as a loving mother anxious for the good of her sons, remain indifferent to the prospect of their dangers, stay silent or pretend not to see or understand the *social conditions which, willingly or not, make difficult or practically impossible a Christian state conforming to the commandments of the Sovereign Lawgiver?"* [20].

But it is not sufficient for the Church to state what is wrong and evil. She wants the temporal order to conform more to God's plan and to the dignity of man [21]. She demands "the setting up of

(18) P.P. XII, Christmas Allocution, 1942, recalled in the Encyclical, Evangelii Praecones, 2nd June 1951, and in the Allocution to Italian Workers, 1st May, 1955.

(19) P.P. XII, Radio Message, Whitsun, 1941. The Pope adds: "On the form given to society, conforming or not to the divine laws, depends and permeates the good or evil of souls."

(20) Radio Message, Whitsun 1941.

(21) P.P. XII, Radio Message, 1st September, 1944.

an economic and social order which will be more in accordance with the *plan and the means to rebuild an abundantly fruitful social structure*" [22].

The broad outlines of the programme were clearly set out by Pope Pius XII in his Christmas message of 1942 :
1. Respect for the dignity of the *human person* and for his rights;
2. Internal *unity* of society and of the family;
3. Nobility of *work* with all its implications for social reforms for the working classes;
4. Far-reaching reconstruction of the *juridical order* for the security of man and the protection of his rights against all arbitrary human intervention;
5. A concept of the *State* at the service of society, of man and of his destiny.

The natural and supernatural order established by God.

It is the duty of Christians to build a world according to the natural and supernatural order designed by God.

God made a moral order for man's good. It is this order which reflects human nature and which God laid down as the basis of man's communal life in time and space. In his very first encyclical, Summi Pontificatus, Pope Pius XII declared the unity of the human race. He declared that it is wonderful to contemplate the human race in the unity of its origin in God : "with the same God, the same Father of us all, Who is above all things, pervades all things and lives in all of us" (Ephes. IV, 6.); in the unity of its *nature* composed, in all, of a body and a spiritual and immortal soul; in the unity of its *immediate end* and its mission in the world; in the unity of its *habitation,* the earth, to the fruits of which all men have a natural right and which can be used to sustain and develop life; in unity of its *supernatural end* which is God Himself, to whom everything must progress in the unity of means to reach this end [23].

---

(22) P.P. XII, Radio Message, 1st June, 1941.
(23) P.P. XII, Encyclical, Summi Pontificatus, 20th October, 1939.

There *is* a natural order, even if its form changes with historical and social developments. Its essential characteristics remain always the same [24] : first, the family and private ownership for man's personal security, then, local institutions and vocational groups as complements to his security and, finally, the State.

Christians should unite with all men of good-will, even those not in the Church's fold, to defend and respect the natural order. We will see further on how Pope Pius XII demanded loyal and effective co-operation for the creation of an economic and social order more in line with the real needs of human nature. This co-operation is also necessary to obtain a more rational and equitable distribution of the world's resources. More than half mankind suffers from a growing hunger and under-developed peoples have urgent and complex problems. The social teaching of the Church, far from opposing the active co-operation of all, positively encourages it to answer the crying needs of mankind.

But when Christians study the relationship between the natural and supernatural orders they should hold fast to the truth and avoid two conflicting errors.

The first error is *to deny the truth of the natural order,* to believe that this order has no intrinsic value, that human nature is inherently evil, to make the natural order depend on supernatural grace for its existence. There is a stability in the natural order because it is based on man, a spiritual being, whose nature is turned towards God. Pius XII said : "the Church has affirmed the value of that which is human and in accordance with nature; without hesitation she has sought it out and developed it. She does not admit that man is only corruption and sin before God. On the contrary, in her eyes, original sin did not intimately affect his qualities and powers and even left essentially intact the natural light of his intelligence and liberty" [25].

The Holy Father also acclaimed modern technical conquests.

---

(24) P.P. XII Christmas Message, 1955.
(25) P.P. XII, Allocution to Congress of Humanistic Studies. 25th September, 1949.

"The Church loves and favours human progress ... all research and all discoveries of the forces of nature made by technical progress are only the search for and the discovery of the greatness, the wisdom and the harmonious design of God"[26].

Finally, the Holy Father, in his Christmas message of 1955, denounced both the error of the modern man who is lost in his pride of human power and his domination of nature and the mistakes of those who shut themselves up in "a disdainful and despairing solitude, suggested by their fear and inability to participate in the life around them".

On the other hand *there is the serious error of looking on the natural order as complete and exclusive in itself.* The natural order must be left open to grace, to the supernatural life which perfects the human order according to the plan laid down by God and also to the life with God by divine adoption, which was brought by Christ to the world.

Man's misfortune to-day is that he sets himself up in his supposed self-sufficiency, revels in his technical and material progress and then misunderstands the limits of human nature. He forgets original sin and its results which have deprived man "not of his domination over the earth but of the guarantee that he can exercise that domination" [27]. He ignores the true meaning of sin, which causes deep and wide disorder in the life of men and of society. He does not know that man can find stability and harmony only in Christ, the Redeemer. A great and unique event occurred in the history of mankind : the Incarnation of the Son of God. The truth and effect of this historical fact should be appreciated by men [28]. Christians, particularly, ought to know that "the Son of

---

(26) P.P. XII, Radio Message, Christmas, 1953.
(27) P.P. XII, Christmas Message, 1956.
(28) "Henceforth mankind cannot repulse and forget the place and habitation of God on earth with impunity, for in the economy of Providence, this is necessary for the establishment of harmony between man and his possessions, and between these and God. St. Paul, the Apostle, described the whole of this order in an admirable synthesis: "It is all for you, and you for Christ, and Christ for God". Whoever would ignore God and Christ from these indestructible groupings and would forget the Apostle's words on man's

God made man is the only solid bastion of humanity, even in its social and historical life, and that in taking on human nature, He confirmed human nature as the basis and rule of that moral order" [29].

It is to these sources, consecrated by the Word of God made man, that Christians should bring back modern society. The source of their faith should equip Christians for the ordering of public life and they have a perfect right to join different institutions and organisations for this end.

In so doing there is no reason to suppose that they are not being true to themselves. On the contrary, they have "no aim but to *serve* the common good in accordance with God's will". They remain open to every good endeavour and to all true progress. They work with those who, obedient to the light of reason, can and should accept Christian teaching, at least in so far as it is founded on the natural law.

Thus Christians should co-operate in the building of a world according to the natural and supernatural order designed by God. The Church, in its social teaching, sets forth the basic principles and evolution of this order. In showing men how to save the world and how to restore the temporal, social and economic order in Christ she does not contradict human nature. On the contrary, she frees men and human society from their self-conceit and thus from the weaknesses of their own limitations. She helps them to recover their natural integrity and to bring the economic and social order back into God's plan. In this way she ensures true consistency and security because "They were all created through him and in him; he takes precedency of all, and in him all subsist" (Col. I, 17)—for as grace purifies man's nature and renders him more truly man, so the Church while respecting the State in its own order, creates the climate which furthers the true accomplishment by the State of its mission as a State.

rights over material things, would bring about a vital break in the Creator's plan". (P.P. XII, Christmas Message, 1955)
   (29) **P.P. XII, Christmas Message, 1955.**

Third Reason : The Church, as the Mystical Body of Christ, has the mission of uniting all men in Christ.

Mankind treasures the memory of its unity which has been broken by sin. Man's history is a record of his progress towards unity despite appearances and notwithstanding upheavals, wars and strife. The story of this struggle towards unity is the real meaning of history.

This too, though on a higher level, is the mission of the Church.

To unite all men, in spite of all that divides them (race, class, language, mentality, civilisation) in a single Body, loved by His divine Spirit; to unite them in the communion of His Life and charity so that they might partake in the unity of the divine nature and the life of the Blessed Trinity; *this* is the sublime design of Jesus Christ for mankind which He expressed in His prayer to His Father "Father that they may be ONE in us . . . "

It is in the Church that this reunion of men redeemed by Christ starts. But it is Christ the Head Who, in His Body, which is the Church, by His divine Spirit brings about this unity so that the body may grow in His charity until all men have come to make up the new man "to the completed growth of Christ" (Ephes. IV, 13) as St Paul said, the Total Christ.

This unity of all men in Christ in the context of history is the third basis of the social teaching of the Church. The Church, through her social doctrine, teaches all men how they should prepare, here and now, to accomplish collectively the destiny of mankind through their thought and action in family, economic, social, national and international planes.

This is also the reason why the Church's social teaching judges those movements which directly or indirectly oppose the fulfilment of God's loving plan for men. It is for this reason in particular (apart from others) that she condemned Nazism and Communism, just as she now denounces the dangers of excessive nationalism.

Finally, if the Popes' work for peace is to be properly understood it must be placed in the perspective of the Church's mission

for the unification of mankind through all the disruptions of history.
"The consciousness of that mission of peace has always shown itself
to be alive and active in the Church, particularly in her Visible
Head, the Roman Pontiff" Pope Pius XII said. This same discourse makes it plain that the Church's social action and teaching
take on their true meaning in the perspective of the last end and
final judgement because it contains this phrase, startling in its
calmness and eschatological import: "If the Church speaks and
passes judgement on present day problems it is in the clear knowledge that she thus anticipates, by virtue of the Holy Spirit, the
sentence which will be confirmed and sanctioned at the end of
time by her Lord and Leader, the Judge of the Universe" [30].

(30) P.P. XII, Radio Message to the World, 24th December, 1951.

III

THE OBJECTIONS

First Objection: The Church's social teaching is an anachronism.

"The social teaching of the Church is out of date to-day. It was designed for a Christian epoch but society has become secular. Modern states organise their own political, economic and social affairs".

Reply: Contrary to what the objection supposes, the social teaching of the Church was worked out in the present epoch precisely to answer the social problems facing modern nations.

One historical fact which has not been heeded enough is very clear. Who was among the first to recognise and respect the autonomy of the temporal order in its own sphere and to define the respective spheres of influence of the Church and the modern State? Surely it was Leo XIII in his encyclical, Immortale Dei, in 1885. The same Pope, six years later, in his encyclical, Rerum Novarum, (1891), set out the essentials of the social teaching in its historical context. It was thus proclaimed that the teaching was designed for the new age when modern society began to emerge.

Far from being old-fashioned, the most striking aspect of the Church's social teaching to the unprejudiced student, is its *up-to-date* quality. Through it the Popes project the light of the natural law, of dogma and of the moral teaching of the Church onto the social problems of their time.

Second Objection: Christian civilisation.

It is said: "The social teaching of the Church advocates a

Christian civilisation. But this concept is unthinkable in our secular age"

Reply: The expression "Christian civilisation" is ambiguous. It can be understood in two ways — one in contradiction to the Church's social teaching and the other in its true sense.

Wrong meaning: That Christian civilisation should be *identifiable* with a particular civilisation at a given time. On the contrary, the doctrine holds that Christianity is bound up with no one civilisation and that it transcends all. Furthermore, not even in the Middle Ages was any civilisation or culture entitled to call itself exclusively Christian or Catholic [31].

Finally, the Pope has also said "no-one dreams of returning to the Middle Ages".

There is a second, and more correct sense, in which a civilisation *which is inspired by* Christianity and in which Christians put their faith into practice in its institutions and public life, can be called a Christian civilisation. Now it is these very principles and ideals affecting the economic, family and social structures which the Church teaches her children in order to guide them. Pope Pius XII demanded that Christians should consider it their principal duty to bring back modern society, in its structures, to the origins consecrated by the Word made Flesh. If Christians ever neglect this duty laid upon them, leaving inert, as far as it depends on them, the law's force for the ordering of public life, they betray their God Who came visibly among us in the stable at Bethlehem [32].

When it is understood that God's plan for mankind is the return of the world to Him in Christ it is easier to understand the

(31) P.P. XII Allocution, 16th May, 1947, at the canonisation of Nicholas of Flue. The Pope shows in what sense the identification of the Middle Ages it held that unity between religion and life was essential. Now this synthesis of unity should be re-made, in every era, by true Christians, if they want to live their faith logically.

(32) P.P. XII, Radio Message, Christmas, 1955.

sense in which the Holy Father can say that those Christians who refuse their mission to bring modern society to God, in Christ, betray Him.

That society is not "sacral", i.e. that the organisation of temporal affairs is no longer made under the authority and in the framework of the Church, is an undisputed historical fact. The Popes have declared that the temporal society is autonomous in its own sphere. But Christians cannot sit back and let society be dominated by materialism, paganism, or atheism which are contrary both to the highest destiny of man and the establishment of a true, lasting and universal civilisation. Christians are not to dominate the world but to serve, love and improve it.

Third objection: Secularism : The States' fear of the Church's encroachment.

The objection runs : "Very well, we recognise that Christians have a duty. But can the modern, secular States avoid seeing a threat to their independence in the social teaching of the Church? Does not this teaching call for a domination of the world by Christ and does it not therefore constitute a new kind of imperialism?"

Reply: No. The modern State has nothing to fear for its authority and the legitimate exercise of its power from the social doctrine of the Church. For this is the doctrine which affirmed the State's right and duty to protect the workers by social legislation in an age when economic liberalism opposed State intervention in the social sphere. This is the social doctrine which teaches that the common welfare is the finest mission of the State in the regulation of society and that the authority of the State must therefore be obeyed.

As to the Church's role in the welfare of human society, it is well to consider the forceful words of Pope Pius XII [33] and to compare the Church's attitude with that of modern imperialism to see how different they are.

(33) Discourse to the Consistory, 20th February, 1946.

Modern imperialism expands over territories conquered by
violence; it seeks to lay hand on the living elements of society and
maintains its grip through external pressure. .

The Church, on the contrary, proceeds quietly. She seeks, first
of all, to win man. *She tries to form the complete man—with his
free co-operation—from within. She prepares him for his responsibilities in society. She moulds man in his capacity as spouse,
parent, worker, citizen, and member of the State.* Indeed the State
is the first to benefit from this educational work which helps it to
carry out its own mission.

Fourth objection: The secularism of the State.

"Many Christians oppose the Church's social teaching because
they defend the secular character of the State and it seems to them
that this teaching does not recognise the State's secular character".

Reply: The expression "Secularism of the State" must be clearly defined if freedom of conscience is not to be gravely compro-
mised.

The secularism of the State can and should be the statement of
its autonomy in its own sphere of the temporal order and in the
exercise of its functions and services in the political, economic,
administrative, judicial, military and educational spheres etc. In
this domain the State has nothing to fear from the Church's
social teaching or action. Quite the contrary, as the Popes have
declared on innumerable occasions. We mentioned earlier that
Leo XIII put forward this principle in the encyclical Immortale
Dei; the French Hierarchy developed it in a detailed declaration
at the Assembly of Cardinals and Archbishops in March, 1945.

But in this same important declaration the French Hierarchy
differentiated between secularism in the correct sense and another
meaning i.e. a philosophical doctrine of secularism by which the
State would impose secularism on men's minds in her schools,
administration and public service to the point where God, His
Gospel and His moral law, would all be denied and efforts made
to present the Church as seeking to dominate modern society. This

anti-religious concept must obviously be opposed by the Church in her social teaching since it undermines freedom of conscience, the State's own mission and true secular character, as well as the rights of God, social peace and national unity. The State's refusal to acknowledge a superior, universal, moral code, founded on the the natural law, leads directly to absolutism as Soviet Russia is now experiencing and as Hitler's Germany did. Peace is constantly imperilled by this absolute independence of the State, which goes so far as to deny any international moral code and, by its aggravation of aggressive nationalism, provokes wars.

Finally, in France, a third meaning is given to the term "State secularism" by those who interpret the law of separation of 1905 in a narrow sense with regard to religion. According to them the formula used in the law: "the Republic does not recognise any religious cult" means that the organisation of the State, the courts and public authorities should completely ignore all religious activity and thus the Church herself.

But the real meaning is quite different [34]. The situation which existed in the *nineteenth* century when religion was considered as a *public service* is no longer in force. But the law, since the separation, does not at all refuse to recognise the existence of the religious authorities. It cannot ignore the fact of religion without denying the daily realities of life. It allows a place to religion, not only in its individual, but also in its institutional and social aspects.

The problem which arises is that of the demands of the *public order* and it is true that differences sometimes arise between Church and State on the meaning of public order because the State holds that she has the right to define her own powers in this sphere.

But the social teaching of the Church can shed most useful light on this matter, particularly as it concerns the common good and the role of the State. A State disposed to respect freedom of conscience would certainly be well advised, in its own interest, not to ignore it.

(34) See the study of M. Coulombel, Professor of law at Nancy, in "la revue trimestrielle de Droit civil," No 1, 1956.

Fifth objection: The social teaching of the Church is addressed only to Christians.

"The social teaching of the Church is limited in its application and can only affect Christians. But it is vitally necessary, if we are to build the earthly City, to have understanding and loyal co-operation between all men of good-will on certain fundamental points acceptable to all".

Reply : Here are the facts :

1. In his major messages throughout the war Pope Pius XII made moving appeals to men of good-will outside the Church for their "loyal and effectual co-operation" in order to create a better judicial order and "to create an economic and social order which would better correspond to the divine law and human dignity" [35].

In the same way, the Pope, in his address to the Catholics of the entire world, June 2nd, 1948, declared : "That they should not hesitate to join their efforts to those of men, who, while they are outside their ranks, are nevertheless in agreement with the social teaching of the Catholic Church..." [36].

2. *The influence of the social teaching of the Church on non-Christians.* The Popes themselves have shown how the social teaching of the Church has been welcomed by men far removed from the Church and has already deeply influenced them.

At the beginning of Quadragesimo Anno Pius XI recalls the considerable repercussions of the encyclical Rerum Novarum in all sectors : it "began little by little to penetrate among those also who, being outside Catholic unity, do not recognise the authority of the Church and thus, Catholic principles of Sociology gradually, became part of the intellectual heritage of the whole human race. Thus, We rejoice that the eternal truths proclaimed so vigorously

(35) P.P. XII, Radio Message, 1st September, 1944.
(36) P.P. XII, Allocution to members of the Sacred College, 2nd June, 1948.

by Our illustrious predecessor are advanced and advocated, not merely in non-Catholic books and journals but frequently also in legislative Assemblies and in courts of justice".

It is important to remember the public tribute paid to the Church's social teaching and to the encyclicals in international meetings and by eminent statesmen [37].

History will one day show how peoples and heads of state were influenced by the powerful Christmas messages of Pope Pius XII and also by his numerous allocutions addressed to representatives of different professions and nationalities. Pope Pius XII thus started a direct method of teaching through personal contact with his listeners. His audiences saw reflected in the Pope's personal and paternal interest in their particular problems the Church's concern to guide all men through the errors and dangers which surround them.

Sixth objection : On the subject of the two-fold source of the Church's social teaching (the natural law and revelation).

It is argued : "Since the Church's social teaching is founded on Revelation how can those who do not believe in this Revelation accept the Church's social teaching?"

(37) It is too often forgotten that one of the former leaders of French Socialism, Albert Thomas, for many years never omitted in his reports to the International Labour Office to pay tribute to the Church's social teaching and its influence in the world. In his report in 1928, the Director of the International Labour Organisation said: "The great movement brought forth by the Catholic Church in Rerum Novarum continues to bear fruit" and he cited documents and facts. In his report of 1929 he concluded his remarks on this point with: "Thus it would appear that the moral force of the Church can powerfully aid the work of social justice". On 14th May, 1931, in a solemn assembly, before the delegates of 50 governments, M. Thomas Cortes paid official tribute on behalf of the I.L.O. to the Encyclical, Rerum Novarum: "In this assembly of working mankind we hear trade-unionists, politicians, and ministers of labour call on Rerum Novarum and, under the active inspiration of its principles, bring us their convinced co-operation. Thus the moral force of the Catholic Church and her spirit of conciliation can forcefully aid the work of international justice and good-will".

Reply : We said earlier that the Church's social teaching is founded on the *natural law*. Now this basis can unite all those who place their confidence in rational human nature. The Church's social teaching appeals to straight reason. It gives a concept of man which can be admired even by those furthest from the Church itself. It defends man's fundamental rights and personal worth. It calls for a human economy, the common good, social justice and brotherly love. How then can it fail to appeal to those who, anguished by the emptiness and futility of other teachings in the face of the overwhelming problems posed by man's own technical and economic progress, feel the need to unite with their fellows to save man and civilisation?

Revelation brings a new light which surpasses but does not extinguish the light of reason. The life of grace embraces the life of nature to transfigure without destroying it. Revelation discloses man's supernatural destiny, God's divine plan for him and the means of his salvation. But Revelation does not contradict the findings of reason and the natural law. It confirms them and guards them against error. To the natural motives for co-operating in the building of a social and economic order she adds others which are imperative for the Christian—motives of faith, of hope and of love of God and of his neighbour. This is what Pope Pius XII underlined in his message of September 1st, 1944, when he appealed to collaborators and comrades in the struggle for the great work of re-construction of a world shaken to its foundations and shattered in its very constitution. Speaking of the Christian ready to work with others in a true spirit of brotherly co-operation, the Holy Father declared : "such a disposition surpasses simple obedience to the moral obligation of civic duties : it raises itself to the dignity of a postulate of conscience, sustained and guided by the love of God and one's neighbour" [38].

Seventh objection : The social teaching of the Church is too rigid in its principles and too vague in their application.

"The social teaching of the Church is made up of unchangeable principles. These are therefore too rigid since life is essentially

(38) P.P. XII, Message of 1st September, 1944.

fluid and the world is continually changing. On the other hand, the principles are too abstract, too remote, too indefinite and too static to give clear and constructive answers to the complex social problems of our age"

Reply : The social teaching of the Church has the characteristic of being both firm in its essential principles and flexible in their application to the needs of each epoch.

Its *principles* remain true for all times and places (concepts of man, of society, and the relationship between them, etc). *Whatever form society takes these principles should always guide Christians whose social life is inspired by their faith.* Furthermore, Pius XII taught us that there is *a natural order in society* (as we have seen); this is the order which must be sought and found among the mists of history and then reconstituted.

"The fundamental, ultimate and ageless laws of society cannot be shattered by an intervention of the human spirit. They can be denied, ignored, scorned and defied but never abrogated. Undoubtedly conditions change with the passage of time ... In any case, through all changes and transformation the end of all social life remains the same, sacred and binding, i.e., the development of the personal attributes of man, made in the image of God. The obligation to realise these unchanging ends rests on every member of the human family no matter what legislator or authority he obeys" [39].

Furthermore, the Church does not want to present men with ready-made solutions. She respects the developments of history, the differences among civilisations and nations, the State's proper sphere of action and individual or collective efforts to build the earthly city. But she requires lay Christians to demonstrate in their actions the principles she gives them.

To help them to find technical solutions the Church, in her social teaching, herself applies the principles to a given era. When we read, for example, the three works of Father Villain on "The

(39) P.P. XII, Message of 24th December, 1942.

Social Teaching of the Church" [40] we see how the author places every problem in the historical perspective of social evolution. The living Magisterium has adopted the applications of unchangeable principles to the changes of each era. In this way both immobility on the one hand and relativeness on the other are avoided. The firmness of the principles takes nothing away from the force and flexibility of their practical application to modern needs.

Pope Pius XII declared in 1945, in speaking of the social teaching of the Church : *"This doctrine, definitely fixed in its fundamental points, is sufficiently wide to be adapted and applied to the changing needs of time provided that this is not to the detriment of its lasting and immutable principles"*[41].

Eighth objection : On the very name "Social Doctrine".

"This social teaching of the Popes does not, properly speaking, constitute a doctrine in the same sense as the term is used to define Marxism, Liberalism, Fascism or the like. It would be more exact to describe it as Christian requirements in social matters".

The doctrine begins with the principles and requirements which form the subject matter of the Magisterium's teaching, but the elaboration of the doctrine no longer devolves on the Church but on everyone who wishes to organize society [42].

Reply : 1) It is true that the word "doctrine" (in relation to the Church's social teaching) has not the same meaning as the word "doctrine" applied to an economic system or a political party. In the latter sense it applies to a technical programme in an exclusively temporal sphere. This is precisely the role that the Church refuses to adopt but leaves to the public and secular powers. 2) When the Hierarchy adheres to the word "doctrine"

(40) Father Villain "L'enseignment social de l'Eglise", Spes.
(41) P.P. XII, Allocution to the Congress of Italian Catholic Action, 29th April, 1945.
(42) Barrère: Revision et developpement du catholicisme social, "Etudes", July — August, 1948, p76.

it is primarily because the abandonment of the traditional term, "social doctrine", would rapidly involve the risk of the abandonment of the very idea of the Church's teaching in social matters. And so, little by little, people would become unaware of the Church's right to have and to teach a social doctrine.

It is also because, — to speak in the most exact language — the term "doctrine" as used by the Church, has a very precise meaning. Etymologically it means, in effect, a teaching (docere). Now the mission of teaching moral and religious truths was entrusted by Jesus Christ to the living Magisterium of His .Church, i.e the Pope and the bishops in communion with him. It is the Magisterium which received the mission to adapt and apply these principles to the social problems of each era.

The answer lies therefore, not in the rejection of the term "social doctrine" but rather in a clear explanation of the word itself as the Church defines it.

CLOSE OF INTRODUCTION

The Church teaches the doctrine and shows its application to human problems. It is with this as inspiration that nations and leaders as well as lay Christians should themselves look for technical solutions for the organisation of temporal society. We have already noticed how the Holy Father appealed to the enterprise, spirit, vision, and courage of Christians and men of good-will. The Church's social doctrine is one of liberation, action and progress.

A significant phrase of Pope Pius XII shows both the reasons for the Pope's intervention and the role that nations and statesmen must *themselves* play in the construction of a better social and economic order [43].

"For Our part, We have made it Our duty, even in the fact of opposition, to warn nations and leaders that after such confusion as this *they will have to build a social and economic order more adequate both to divine law and human dignity,* thus closely uniting all the conditions necessary for true justice and the Christian principles which provide the sole guarantee for salvation, good and peace for all".

This is a wonderful definition of the Church's social teaching and of the benefits it can give to the world if the Christians who have confidence in their Church and fully believe in the mystery of the Redemption know how to understand its application, discover its meaning and help towards its extension, despite those who consider it old-fashioned, narrow and useless.

Our study will be divided into three parts.

The social teaching of the Church brings to the world :

1) A concept of man.

2) A concept of social economy.

3) A concept of human community.

(43) Letter of 14th July, 1945, to M. Charles Flory.

This pastoral letter will confine itself to the first two concepts: that of man and of the social economy. The third extends into international problems and, because of its magnitude, needs a separate study.

PART ONE

A CONCEPT OF MAN

The concept of man which the social teaching of the Church brings to the world is founded on three essential principles.

1) the dignity of the human person;

2) the fundamental equality of men ;

3) the inalienable rights of man who is the subject, not the object of these rights.

We will study each of these three principles in turn and we will indicate how the Popes applied each of them.

First Principle:

THE DIGNITY OF THE HUMAN PERSON

On the 4th February, 1956, Pope Pius XII received in audience the delegates to an international conference on human relations in industry. Referring to the responsibilities of employers, he said, *"Every man has an absolute and transcendent value because the Author of human nature gave him an immortal soul"*.

Setting out the ruling principles which should guide the social reconstruction of the world, Pope Pius XII demanded, (while the war was still on) that everyone should *"render to the human person the dignity conferred on it by God from its creation"* [(44)].

According to the social teaching of the Church, society is at the service of the human person to respect his dignity and allow him to attain his end and his full human development. *"Society is made for man and not man for society"* [(45)].

Pius XI, who proclaimed this daring maxim, explains it in his encyclical. It does not mean that society should be subordinate to the selfish use of the individual but that man is a *social being by nature* and can fully develop his attributes only in society thanks to the help it provides for his physical, intellectual, moral, family and social life. In other words, man is a human person who will realise his full autonomy in communion with others and in co-operation with the other members of society.

Agreement is possible with all those who, even though outside the Church, are determined to defend the *fact* of man's dignity against the dictatorship of totalitarian states.

But differences arise about the *nature* of that dignity. The

(44) Pope Pius XII, Radio Message, 24th December, 1942
(45) Pope Pius XI, Encyclical, Divini Redemptoris.

Church has her own concept : she gives human dignity a fundamental and unshakable basis.

What gives man his dignity? It is the fact that he was created
in the image of God. "The dignity of man is the dignity of the
image of God" said Pius XII in his Christmas message of 1944.
Open the Bible at the story of Creation : (Genesis I, 26). "God
created man in his *own image: he created him in the image of
God*".

What is the meaning of that stupendous truth revealed by God
Himself in Sacred Scripture and inscribed by Him in man's nature?

Two texts of Pope Pius XII help us to understand it : "Thus
one can hope to see emerge more clearly the authentic image of
man, *master not only of things but, above all, of himself, and conscious of his transcending, individual and social destiny and of his
responsibilities as a creature made in God's likeness*"[46].

"*Man is primarily a spirit created in the image of God, responsible for his actions and his destiny, capable of governing himself
and thus finding his greatest dignity*" [47].

Created in the image of God means at the outset that man is
"master of things"; he dominates the things of creation and
inferior beings (animals, plants, etc.) rather as God rules the world.
God gave man the earth and a share of His divine government so
that, depending on his Creator, man could fulfil the creation and
the universe. This is the explicit teaching of the Bible [48].

But why has man this power to dominate other created things?
It is because he is *free* while lesser creatures are not. He is "master

(46) Pope Pius XII, Discourse to the Congress of European-American
Associations, 18th September, 1955.
(47) Pope Pius XII, Replying to the Respects of the Diplomatic Corps,
4th March, 1956.
(48) "And God said, Let us make man, wearing our own image and likeness; let us put him in command of the fishes in the sea, and all that flies
through the air, and the cattle, and the whole earth. . . ." Gen. 1. 26.

of himself" says the Pope in the texts which we study, and *"responsible for his actions and his destiny"*.

But what is the root of this freedom and this responsibility? It is his spirit, the immortal soul he has received from his Creator, his intelligence, reason and will which enable him to think, to choose and to govern himself *as a human being*. "Man" says Pope Pius XII, in another text [49] *"is a personal being, endowed with intelligence and free will; a being who has the final choice of what he will or will not do"*. He is made in the image of God, a being supremely personal and absolutely free.

In the end, what gives man his human dignity, is the fact that he is "conscious of his overriding destiny" and "responsible for his actions and his destiny": it is the realisation that he has been made in God's likeness to imitate God's perfection, His goodness, and His love and mercy for men [50]. He must use his intelligence and will to discover the true significance of his destiny and his actions. He must lift himself up to God to participate, as God has ordained, as brother of Jesus Christ and with Him and by Him, in life eternal in the divine Life of God and of the Blessed Trinity. *This* is man's destiny! "Man" says Pius XII "is the image of God, One and threefold, himself also a person, brother of the man-God Jesus Christ and with Him and by Him, the inheritor of eternal life; this is his true dignity" [51].

The basis of the dignity of the human person is therefore God Himself. It is on Him it rests and He is the reason that it is impregnable. It depends on Him. Man's supreme dignity and true freedom is found in the realisation and loving acceptance of his filial dependence. He thus freely pays homage in adoration, love and submission to the Divine Will.

If this dependence on God constitutes the greatness of man it

---

(49) Pope Pius XII, Allocution to the Sixth International Congress on Criminal Law, repeated in the Discourse to the International Commission of Police, 15th October, 1954.

(50) "But you are to be perfect, as your heavenly Father is perfect" Matt. V. 48. "Be merciful, then, as your Father is merciful". Luke VI. 36.

(51) Pope Pius XII, Allocution to Fiat employees, 31st October, 1948

is because his *dignity, based only on God, depends on none other than God. Man is not subject to earthly things, neither to progress, to the machine, to money nor to technical progress. It is religion and not the perfection of the organisation or of the equipment which gives the worker his dignity* [(52)].

Modern man thinks he can do without God. He rejects this divine basis of his dignity, for him the supreme being is not God, it is man himself. As a result we have "The drama of atheistic Communism" which has so deeply influenced history [(53)]. "We are in the process of proving by experiment that where there is no God neither is there man...... in truth, there is no longer man because there is nothing which surpasses man".

THE APPLICATIONS OF THE PRINCIPLE

Perhaps there are those who think that principles are undoubtedly noble and desirable things but that they cannot be put into practice. As an example, and a complete reply, let us look at some of the applications to which Leo XIII himself put this principle of human dignity in his encyclical, Rerum Novarum.

"...No-one may violate with impunity this dignity of man that God Himself treats with great respect".

There is a striking contrast between God's respect for human dignity and the attitude of too many human beings towards their subordinates......It will be noted that the prohibition is explicit and universal: *"No-one may violate"* ...... If this rule were applied wherever authority is excercised, in all public bodies, in factories and mines, workshops and offices and also in the family, towards employees and servants, it is certain that there would be a new atmosphere throughout the country. Many of those who bear the

(52) Pope Pius XII, "Neither work alone nor the most perfect organisation nor the most powerful equipment are capable of forming and ensuring the dignity of the worker, only religion and all that is ennobled and sanctified by it can do this ! " Allocution to Fiat employees, 31st October, 1948.
(53) Father de Lubac "Le Drame de l'Humanisme Athèe" p. 62.

heavy responsibility of authority still do not realise that the most important thing for the servant, the agricultural or industrial workers, the employee, or the client is to be respected as a human person.

Leo XIII continues…"As to the rich and the employers, they must never treat the worker as a slave; in him they must respect the dignity of a man, enhanced by the dignity of a Christian…… It is shameful and inhuman to use men as mere instruments of providing lucre and of reckoning their value only in terms of the strength of their arms".

It is difficult to imagine to-day the shock these forceful words of the Head of the Church produced over sixty years ago. It was the formal condemnation of a practice only too common at the time. Leo XIII here lays down a moral rule of conduct valid for all time.

………"It is forbidden for masters to impose work on their subordinates which is beyond their capacity or unsuitable for their age or sex".

From this vigorous prohibition, which still remains relevant, as well as from the important efforts of political and trade union movements, has sprung legislation to control the work of women and children and to limit the number of working hours.

Pius XI, in Quadragesimo Anno, noted the influence of Rerum Novarum on labour legislation. "From this persevering effort a new right was born, which the previous century had completely ignored. *This was an assurance for workers of the respect they are entitled to as of right as men and as Christians;* e.g. their health, and well-being, family, accommodation, work-shops, wages, insurance against occupational risks, in a word, everything which affects the condition of the workers and particularly, of women and children, is the subject of this protective legislation."

Pius XII explicitly states that the doctrine and social standpoint of Leo XIII are founded on the principle of man's supreme destiny. "There is no doubt that the statement of man's supreme destiny constitutes the heart of the teaching of Leo XIII on labour questions" [54].

In the same trend, Pius XII, speaking on the Church's social teaching, to the workers at the Fiat plant of Turin, explained that the social reforms that she advocates are inspired by the principle of the dignity of the human person.: "If the Church, in her social teaching, always insists on *due regard for the innate dignity of man;* if she demands a just wage for the worker in his contract of employment; if she exacts adequate assistance for him in his spiritual and material needs, surely the reason is that *the worker is a human being* and his capacity for work should not therefore be considered as mere *'merchandise'* !......."

(54) Pope Pius XII, Allocution to the Christian Associations of Italian Workers, 14th May, 1953.

Second principle.

FUNDAMENTAL EQUALITY OF MEN

To the first principle, of the dignity of the human person, the Church relates a second on the fundamental equality of men. Because every human being, no matter how lowly his social position, possesses this dignity there exists between men an innate equality.

On the subject of this dignity Leo XIII said: *"From this point of view all men are equal; there is no difference between rich and poor, masters and servants, rulers and subjects"* [55].

1. THE PRINCIPLE.

Notwithstanding differences of age, position or physical, intellectual or moral attributes there exists a fundamental equality in nature. "All men share one and the same origin in the order of nature. [56] : they possess the same human nature the dignity of which is stated and defended by the Church.

Above and beyond this natural equality, which everyone, even the unbeliever, can acknowledge, the Church teaches that Christians share a higher equality in the supernatural order. They share the same faith and hope, the same destiny, the same Baptism and sacraments, the same Eucharist......all have been ransomed by Christ and admitted to the same table......all are members of one and the same body. And it is the same Spirit which united this body in a single love. All have been adopted by the same Father in Heaven. All are called to become sons by the Son in a single family, the family of the children of God, which is the Church.

(55) Leo XIII, Rerum Novarum.
(56) Leo XIII, In plurimis.

II. THE RESULTS AND PRACTICAL
CONSEQUENCES OF THIS PRINCIPLE

Unbelievers, and perhaps some nominal Christians, are doubt-less tempted to neglect the second, supernatural aspect of the equal-ity of men because this domain is strange to them. They should make the effort to see the practical results of such a principle on a Christian who is determined to live his faith and to love Christ sincerely! This principle, rather than that of natural equality, is the basis of the brotherhood of man.

Saint Paul himself pointed out the practical consequences in decisive terms: *"No more Jew or Gentile, no more slave and free-man, no more male and female; you are all one person in Jesus Christ"*. [57]; an innate equality beyond all distinctions of race, nationality, position and sex. *"We too, all of us, have been baptised into a single body by the power of a single Spirit, Jews and Greeks, slaves and free men alike; we have all been given drink at a single source, the one Spirit"* [58]. The innate equality of all men in Christ transcends secondary and artificial differences which set men against each other and also the natural differences between them.

The practical effect of this principle can be verified by the history of the early Christian communities. "There was one heart and soul in all the company of believers; none of them called any of his possessions his own, everthing was shared in common" [59].
Slavery could no longer be maintained in the face of this principle. The early Christians, applying the principle, shared all that they had, as religious orders and congregations do today, without dis-tinctions of class, position or family background.

On the social plane, Leo XIII drew important consequences for the behaviour of masters to their servants from these two first principles: "It was ordained that masters should recognise the human dignity of their servants and treat them accordingly; not to consider servants *as having a different nature to their masters'*

(57) Gal. III. 28.
(58) I. Cor. XII, 13.
(59) Acts. IV. 32.

but, on the contrary, the same one; both have, in effect, the same religion and serve the same God" [60].

These are the same principles that the Popes call on to *establish better human relations* between employers and workers, masters and subordinates. Pope Pius XII said that *the equal human dignity of all,* which for its part, results entirely from the transcendental end common to all inspires them [61]. And again; "For the Church, all men are equal in dignity before God; they ought therefore to be equal also in the free or necessary relationships which unite them" [62].

The Pope, going beyond the framework of labour relations, judges the great weaknesses of the social order in the light of these same principles. "The great *weakness of the social order is that it is neither deeply Christian nor truly human but merely material and economic and that it does not rely on that which should be its basis and the solid foundation of its unity, i.e. the character common to men by nature and that of sons of God by divine adoption"* [63].

On the international plane the third part of this treatise will deal with the repercussions of the same principles on relations between nations. The principle of the fundamental equality of men and the text of Saint Paul (neither Jews nor Gentiles) condemn the *racial segregation* of certain countries to-day as well as the Nazi thesis of the superiority of the Aryan race. In this context it is useful to re-read the encyclical of Pius XI which condemns, in Nazism particularly, "the error of speaking of a national God, a national religion" which claim to imprison God, Creator of the universe, King and Law-giver of all nations, "within the frontiers

(60)   Leo XIII, Encyclical, In plurimis.
(61)   Pope Pius XII, Allocution to the Christian Association of Italian Workers, 14th May, 1953.
(62)   Pope Pius XII, Allocution of 4th February, 1956, to the International Congress on Human Relations in Industry.
(63)   Pope Pius XII, Allocution to members of the Christian Union of the leaders of Italian Industry, 31st January, 1952.

of a single people, in the *narrow confines* of a community of the blood of a single race" [64].

To sum up, Pius XII called for "the recognition of the equality of all in the inviolability of personal rights" [65].

III

NATURAL AND SOCIAL INEQUALITIES CONTRASTED WITH THE PRINCIPLE OF THE EQUALITY OF MEN

It is a fact that inequalities exist between men which seem to be in complete contradiction to the principle of innate equality. These inequalities come from different causes and are of varying importance. For the sake of clarity we will divide them into different categories.

There are, first of all, *individual* inequalities; human beings are born with differences of sex, health, physique, intelligence and talents. (1st category).

Other inequalities spring from diversity *of functions* (2nd category) called for by the organisation of society. Every nation must have men to fill public office and others to carry on the different professions necessary or useful for the common good and these callings all require different aptitudes and qualities.

There is also the inequality of *condition,* (3rd category), in the possession of intellectual advantages, fortune and social position which arises from a difference of temperament or talents. Gifted men often succeed in obtaining high positions although they started in very modest circumstances. But, of course there are also those who succeed more because of inherited wealth and family influence than because of merit.

In the fourth category can be grouped the inequalities which

(64) Pius XI, Encyclical, Mit Brennender Sorge, 1937.
(65) Pope Pius XII, Christmas Message, 1949.

are the result of the *sins of individuals;* unscrupulous and inhuman profiteers, who get on by every means, lawful and unlawful.

Finally, apart from inequalities created by individuals, there are inequalities arising from the disorder of society and the unfair distribution of the wealth of the world (5th category).

What is the Church's teaching on these inequalities?

Faced with the inequalities of the *first category*, springing from nature the Church tries to discover God's design.

As far as the inequalities of the *sexes* is concerned the Church's social teaching is very full and lays down the exact sense in which it exists. She affirms the fundamental rights of women as being equal to those of men as far as their *personal dignity* is concerned : "in their personal dignity, as children of God, man and woman are *absolutely equal*" [66]... "as far as personality is concerned they are entitled to equal honour, dignity, worth and respect" [67]. The Church was the principal emancipator of woman from her degrading and unnatural slavery.

But it is the natural order itself which obliges us to recognise the natural diversity of gifts, character and temperaments in man and woman. "Certain (of these) are proper only to man and others only to woman or they are unequally distributed, some being more developed in man and others in woman, *because nature has given each a different sphere of activity and a distinct rôle to play* [67]. The particular characteristics which distinguish the sexes have repercussions in family and community life. It is not possible to reverse this natural order "without nature herself always intervening to re-establish it" [68]. And the Pope, speaking of the awakening of nature thus thwarted asks : "it remains to be seen

(66) Pope Pius XII, Allocution to Italian women, 21st October, 1945.
(67) Pope Pius XII, Allocution to girl members of Catholic Action, 24th April, 1943.
(68) Pope Pius XII, Allocution to Italian women, 21st October, 1945.

if a readjustment (or reform) of the present social structure will not be brought about some day" [69].

Even though, in general, nothing can be done about the other inequalities of the first category, the Church's social doctrine repeats the great principle of the respect of the human person, no matter what its weaknesses or its disabilities of childhood or old age. We know with what solicitude the Church surrounds children, the sick, the poor and the old and sets up social institutions to help, support and protect them.

The inequalities of the *second category* (arising from differences in functions and callings in society), are recognised by the Church as useful and good, once justice and charity are respected. They are, *in themselves*, a good thing from the point of view of society. "This inequality operates for the benefit of all, individuals and society alike. Social life requires various qualities and different duties in its organisation" [70]. These inequalities arising from different duties are not themselves an obstacle. "In a people worthy of the name all inequalities which spring, not from mere caprice, but from the very nature of things : i.e. inequalities of culture, of possessions, and of social position (without prejudice, naturally, to justice and mutual charity), are no obstacle to a true community spirit and brotherly love" [71]. The organic concept of society, borrowed from Saint Paul's image of the body—the body whose unity implies the diversity of functions for the individual and common good—explains, in the Church's social doctrine, the importance and usefulness she sees in the diversity of tasks. Discovering their need of each other men are led to help and love each other and to collaborate for the common good of society.

Faced with the inequalities of the *third category* (culture, pos-

(69) Pope Pius XII, Allocution to girl members of Catholic Action, 24th April, 1953. The Pope took a complete programme of thought and action from these principles.

The texts fill a book called "The Feminine Problem" in the collection of "Papal Teachings" brought out by the monks of Solesmes.

(70) Leo XIII, Rerum Novarum.

(71) Pope Pius XII, Message of 24th December, 1944.

sessions and standard of living) the Church offers a positive programme which tends to diminish them progressively. It does so,
first of all by the practical respect for everybody's fundamental
rights, particularly the "right to sustain and develop the corporal,
intellectual and moral life" (Pius XII), the right of every citizen to
"a certain level of intellectual, moral and physical culture" (Pius
XI in the encyclical Divini illius Magistri) and the right of
use of material goods; presupposing the right to acquire property. It does so by the operation of the doctrine of the common
good and of the demands of social justice and charity, and
ultimately, by the application of this doctrine on the universal
distribution of worldly goods.

The inequalities of the *fourth category* (fruits of men's sin and
malice) are severely condemned by the social doctrine of the
Church. Pius XI denounced these "profiteers, more or less numerous, who know, thanks to the power of money and organisation,
how to gain a privileged position over others" [72]. Already in his
encyclical, In Plurimis, Leo XIII had described the disastrous
effects of sin on the brotherly community of men; "all evils derive
from original sin and notably that monstrous perversity by which
there have been men who, forgetting their common origin with
their brothers, instead of practising good-will and mutual respect,
have listened only to their passions and begun to consider other
men as being their inferiors and to treat them, in consequence, as
animals born to the yoke" [73].

Finally, the inequalities of the *fifth category* pose the problems
of the *wrongful distribution of wealth*. There are few subjects
which have received more attention from the Popes. They have
all passed judgement on the social inequalities due to the present
disorders of society and the economic system.

Leo XIII, at the beginning of Rerum Novarum, noted "the
enormous fortunes of some few individuals, and the utter poverty
of the masses".

(72) Pius XI, Quadragesimo Anno.
(73) Leo XIII, Encyclical, In Plurimis, 5th May, 1888.

Forty years afterwards Pius XI forcefully declared that "the immense number of proletarians on the one hand, and the enormous wealth of the very rich on the other, are an unanswerable argument that the material goods so abundantly produced in this age of industrialism are far from rightly distributed and equitably shared among the various classes of men" [74].

Pius XII came back time and time again to this problem which preoccupied him. He drew attention to the growing number of workers who come up against wealthy interests which, under cover of their remoteness, succeed in totally neglecting their social duty and make it almost impossible for the worker to have anything for himself [75].

The Pope said that "a more just distribution of wealth is, and remains, a main point of the programme of Catholic social doctrine" [76]. That there should be, within certain limits, an unequal division of the goods of the earth in the natural course of things is a fact neither economically nor socially abnormal. "But", continues the Pope, "the Church opposes the accumulation of this wealth in the hands of a comparatively small number of very rich men while great classes are condemned to pauperism and an economic condition unworthy of human beings".

We will see, in the second part of this study, the remedies prescribed by the Church to correct this economic and social disorder. It is sufficient to note here that the principle reason that the Church *rises against* this unjust inequality is the same principle of the fundamental equality of men. It is obvious how relevant this social doctrine is and what a great influence it must have on any analysis of the social state and the urgent reforms needed, particularly for the betterment of the general populace and the improvement of the workers' lot.

(74) Pius XI, Quadragesimo Anno.
(75) Pope Pius XII, Radio-Message, 1st September, 1944.
(76) Pope Pius XII, Allocution to Italian Catholic Action, 7th Sept, 1947.

Third principle

THE INALIENABLE RIGHTS OF MAN, WHO IS THE SUBJECT AND NOT THE OBJECT OF THESE RIGHTS

I. — THE PRINCIPLE :
MAN IS A SUBJECT AND NOT A MERE OBJECT

Man is not a mere *object* which can be disposed of like an inanimate agent or some sort of tool. But this is what in fact happens too often. "In many of the most important activities of his life he has been reduced to a *mere object* of society" [77]. This error has been frequently denounced by Pius XII. Material goods are not the only object of political speculations between nations — man too is used, "man lowered in so many cases to the level of a piece of raw material" [78]. The Popes have condemned the liberal economy and Communist socialism in turn because both, for different reasons, looked on man as an object at the service of the economy. Pius XII spoke out against systems which do not protect the personal dignity of workers and "make their productive capacity a *mere object* which 'society' can fully exploit at its pleasure and will" [79].

Man is not an object; he is a subject, a subject by right. This expression is often found in the writing of Pius XII. It calls for the recognition and practical respect of the dignity of the human person and his rights, in social relations, in the life of the national economy and before the law. It is, for men, "the demand, legitimate in itself, to be considered and treated, not as objects but as subjects of the social life, particularly in the State and national economy" [80].

(77) Pope Pius XII, Christmas Message, 1952.
(78) Pope Pius XII, Allocution to members of the Congress on International Exchange, 7th March, 1948.
(79) Pope Pius XII, Allocution to employees of the Fiat works in Turin, 31st October, 1948.
(80) Pope Pius XII, Christmas Radio Message, 1950.

In the social relations between employers and workers and for the discussion of working agreements "the practical statement that man is the subject and not the object of social relations" provides the essential aim of trade unions, which is "to protect the individual against impersonal business interests which do not accept their social responsibility" [80].

In dealing with the national economy Pius XII calls on the same principle to defend the right and liberty of men, who feel themselves closely united because of the "objective" goal of the social economy, to organise themselves in such a way that "the social order of the economy, far from attacking their freedom in the choice of means adapted to this end, will guarantee and protect it. This holds equally good for every kind of worker, whether self-employed or not, for with regard to the end of the social economy, every producing member is the *subject* and not the object of the economic life" [81]. This rule, to which we shall return, explains an idea dear to Pius XII; all those who, in no matter what capacity, are involved in the social economy have the right to make their voices heard in the organisation of that economy. They should be able to contribute their suggestions, ideas, and experience to bring about desirable improvements for they are free *subjects*, intelligent and active.

Finally, *"before the law"*. If the science of law has justice and injustice for its object, *"the subject* to which these rules of law are directed is man, the human person" [82].

In the same way in plans and laws—"Every plan or programme should be inspired by the principle that man as *subject*, guardian and promoter of human values is more important than material things and the implications of technical progress" [83].

(80) Pope Pius XII, Message of 24th December, 1952.
(81) Pope Pius XII, Allocution to members of the Congress on International Exchange, 7th March, 1948.
(82) Pope Pius XII, Discourse to Italian Catholic jurists, 6th Nov. 1949.
(83) Pope Pius XII, Message of 24th December, 1952.

II. — THE FUNDAMENTAL RIGHTS OF MAN

"Man, as a person, possesses rights which he holds from God, which should remain, in the face of society, immune from all attacks which tend to deny, abolish or neglect them" [84]. The Church thus defends the rights of man, which are inscribed in human nature and which come from God, the author of that nature. The Church protects the fundamental rights of man against attack from all quarters. "In her eyes these essential rights are so inviolable that, against them, no reason of State, no pretext of the common good can prevail. They are protected by an unsurmountable barrier" [85].

Pius XII shows in the same passage, the considerable effect that this principle would have in the world if it were universally respected. "If this principle were respected how many tragic catastrophes and menacing dangers would be averted! By itself, it could renew the social and political physiognomy of the earth."

The fundamental rights of the human person

Pius XII listed the fundamental rights of the human person [86]. We will consider in particular those which affect the social problem directly : the right to the use of material goods and the right to work.

---

(84) Pius XI, Encyclical on Nazism.
(85) Pope Pius XII, Allocution to members of the Congress on Humanistic Studies, 25th September, 1949.
(86) Christmas Message, 1942: "The right to maintain and develop physical, intellectual and moral life, and in particular the right to a religious training and education; the right to worship God, both in private and in public, including the right to engage in religious works of charity; the right, in principle, to marriage and to the attainment of the purpose of marriage, the right to wedded society and home life; the right to work as an indispensable means for the maintenance of family life; the right to the free choice of a state of life, and therefore of the priestly and religious state; the right to a use of material goods, subject to its duties and to its social limitations."
Some of these rights are, at present, violated in certain totalitarian States. In other documents the Pope added political rights, like the right of association, the right to juridical security, the right to publish the truth and the right to life itself which are also frequently violated.

First right : "Right to material possessions".

" The right to the use of material possessions with the aware-ness of their proper use and social limitations".

Objection : An objection is immediately raised. "A doctrine which defends the right of private property has no hope of appeal-ing to the masses. Once it states this right it appears as the pro-tector of owners and consolidates both the privileges of wealth and the social inequalities which flow from them".

Reply : 1) If properly understood, this doctrine, on the con-trary, *answers the deepest aspirations of the masses.* How many working-class families long to have a place of their own with, per-haps, a little property and basic security? This doctrine is the positive sign of how a man can better himself and his family.

2) When it is closely studied it becomes clear that this is a *very bold doctrine for it implies, in effect, a complete transforma-tion of the economic society.* The right is affirmed for all, includ-ing the most wretched and poor. In effect it means the disappear-ance of the proletariat, that is, of those who have nothing and who live in complete insecurity.

3) This reform, ensuring the respect for a certain right to private ownership, is so necessary that the Socialist International proclaimed it in its Statutes of 1951 [87]. Even in Soviet Russia the last few years have seen an important evolution, in the sector of the small private holding [88].

----

(87) The Socialist International "recognises that Socialist planning is compatible with the continuation of private ownership in certain important sectors, and particularly in small and medium sized enterprises."

(88) See Chambre's "Le Marxisme en Union Sovietique" Chap. III: Right of ownership and management. Capitalist ownership has been comp-letely liquidated in the U.S.S.R. But alongside State and the communal ownership of the Kolkhozien, Russian law recognises a "personal" owner-ship which covers individual consumer goods and things like gardens, homes and tools. The owner cannot use them to exploit the work of others but the règime was forced to break its rigid principles to concede at least this mea-sure of private ownership.

To sum up, the extension of the workers' holding of some private property is an important claim in the social teaching of the Church. "The dignity of the human person normally demands the right to the use of earthly goods as a natural foundation for a livelihood, and to that right corresponds the fundamental obligation to grant private property, as far as possible, to all [89].

Now economists foresee a revolution, already begun, in the notion of respect and protection for the small holding which corresponds to the needs and work of the human person. "In both capitalist and collectivist regimes" writes Father Bigo [90], "an evolution of primary importance is taking shape, which tends to recognise the right to a certain amount of private property". On the basis of a criterion that is not only material but also human the author distinguishes property of the first and property of the second degree, according to its relation to man's need and work. While the latter is more and more submitted to collective authority, the former, because it is linked to the needs of family life and personal work, is respected. It has been re-established and promoted : "an effort is made to extend it to new sections of the population so as to afford the individual at least his minimal living space" [91].

Far from being out of date, the Church's social teaching has, in fact, led the way on this point.

Principles of the Right of Ownership.

The Church's social teaching on the right of ownership can be summed up in the following principles.

First principle: that the resources of creation are destined for all and the goods of the earth are meant to be shared.

(89) Pope Pius XII, Christmas Message, 1942.
(90) Father Bigo, "Marxisme et Humanisme" p. 235.
(91) Father Bigo, do. p. 275.

All the natural fruits of the earth belong in common and to the whole human race without distinction. God created them for all men and they are at the disposal of all according to the principles of justice and charity. They should serve for the good of all and to give better living conditions to those who have need of them.

The first and fundamental right, which concedes in principle the use of earthly goods to all, dominates and enlightens this whole doctrine of ownership. It is particularly bold and far-reaching and implies applications that the Popes themselves have mapped out in certain spheres.

On the international plane this principle is the basis of the brotherhood of nations in the use of the world's riches for the betterment of humanity. Pius XII denounced the imbalance between the creditor and debtor nations [92]. There are irritating discrepancies in the standards of living of different people which the brotherhood of nations demands should disappear. In the name of the fundamental principle of the sharing by all in the goods of the earth Pius XII condemned "the narrow calculations of egoists, tending to corner economic resources and the materials of common use so that the nations less favoured by nature remain outside" [93]. A true application was also made by Pius XII to the sad problem of immigrants [94]. "As long as the earth offers, anywhere, the means of feeding a great multitude" a State, having received certain guarantees, cannot refuse without just and reasonable cause, access to its territories to strangers who are destitute. It is necessary to bring about "a better distribution of men on the face of the earth that God created and prepared for the use of all" [95].

Within a single nation, in the name of the same principle, the Popes call on men to relate the distribution of the world's resour-

(92) Pope Pius XII, Allocution to the members of the International Labour Office, 25th March, 1949.
(93) Pope Pius XII, Christmas Message, 1951.
(94) Pope Pius XII, Letter to Most Reverend Mgr. Nicholas, Archbishop of Cincinatti, 24th December, 1948.
(95) Pope Pius XII, Radio Message, 1st June, 1941.

ces to the needs of the common good and the norms of social justice [96]. If, as we have seen, they condemn the excessive disproportion between the gross fortunes of a few and the miserable lives of many and if they call for a more equitable distribution of wealth it is in order that "the goods, created by God for all men, should belong to all equitably" [97].

Thus the same principle is invoked for a wider distribution of private ownership. Pius XII showed the link between private ownership and the fundamental principle that the world's goods are destined for all [98]. The extension of ownership to all men would make it possible for all to excercise their right to the use of material goods [99]. The right of private ownership, which comes in second place, is a means of realising the primary and fundamental right.

Second principle: the distinction between the right of ownership and use.

THE RIGHT

The owner has a *true* right over his property. It is *a natural* right, i.e. men receive it from nature and thus from God, in so far as human nature has been created by God and is His work. It is therefore a requirement of a human being who, because he is rational and free, can and should wisely organise the use of goods necessary for his own needs and those of his family, not only in the present but for the future, which implies the right to possess them. If a man holds this right from nature it is therefore not derived from

(96) Pius XI, Encyclical, Quadragesimo Anno.
(97) Pope Pius XII, Letter, Sertum Laetitiae, 1st November, 1939.
(98) Pope Pius XII, Message of 1st June, 1941.
(99) Pius XI, in Quadragesimo Anno, "that by means of it (private ownership) the goods which the Creator has destined for the whole human race may truly serve this purpose. Now these ends cannot be secured, unless some definite and stable order is maintained".

the State. He can excercise it as much over consumer goods as over means of production [100].

THE USE OF PROPERTY

But the Church's doctrine makes a distinction between this right of disposing and of administering goods and the use to which they can be put by the owner. According to this doctrine the owner can use them freely for a legitimate end, which is, in this case, a community end. Their use is subordinate to a moral law which is binding on the conscience of the owner. Ownership is not, as the civil law says, the right to enjoy and dispose of things absolutely freely, within the limit of the law which prevents damage to others. He who owns something is truly its master. But this master is not, as Turgot would have it, "the absolute master of his property". He is not free to enjoy it egotistically, solely to satisfy his personal whim and for his exclusive benefit. In the use he makes of it he should, on his own responsibility, take into account the fact that the world's goods are intended for the benefit of all and for the use of all.

Ownership is not a social function at the service of the State since it springs from a personal right which the State itself should respect and protect. But it *has* a social function; it is subordinate to the common good. It is a right which entails social obligations. The principle of riches was clearly stated by Saint Thomas "Man should not consider his material possessions as his own, but as *common to all*, so as to share them without hesitation when others are in need" (IIa, IIae, q. 66, a. 2).

A bold principle : riches are intended for the use of the community; they should be used to assist those in need. There is un-

---

(100) Pope Pius XII, Message of 1st September, 1944. In this passage the Pope affirms the right of ownership over the means of production as well as over consumer goods against those systems which deny the principle or render it impossible in practice. But the Pope did not intend by this to accept any concept of private ownership; shortly afterwards, in the same text, he condemns, **as contrary to the natural law,** that form of capitalism which, founded on erroneous ideas, takes to itself an unlimited right of ownership without any reference to the common good.

doubtedly no chapter of the Church's social teaching which is less known. There are even Christians who do not know that their religion obliges them in conscience to examine the source of their income, the use they make of it, the placing of their capital and they way they use their property. They feel they have done their duty by giving a few coppers to the street-beggar or putting a few pieces of silver on the collection plate [101].

The masses too are under a misapprehension when they accuse the Church of condoning the materialism of money and of covering up by approval or silence, the abuse of wealth.

The Church's social teaching distinguishes two cases :

First case : in the normal way in the ordinary course of life.

Once one has enough for the necessities and reasonable comforts of life there is a duty to give out of what is superfluous to the poor [102]. The duty is one of Christian charity on which we will be judged at the Last Judgement and is not an optional concession or favour showing outstanding generosity.

Of course the idea of "superfluous" is delicate to pin down. What *is* important is that we should be constantly aware of this point. The conscience should be tuned in to the moral law, which it can interpret by the Holy Spirit, Whose love marks the new regime instituted by Christ. We can only hope that through the movements of Catholic Action the laity themselves will provide some practical yard-stick to measure this question.

But the principle is clear : all that is necessary to bring up and provide for a family in decent comfort, in keeping with its social position, (keeping in mind the necessary reaction of Christians against paganising and excessively expensive habits arising from the pressure to comply with popular fashions and standards) must first be put to onc side.

(101) Article of Father Bigo, "Richesse et évangile" in the Revue de l'Action Populaire, March 1956.
(102) Leo XIII, Rerum Novarum.

Apart from all that is thus necessary, the *whole* of the residue should be placed at the disposal of those who are in need in the name of charity, (love of God and our neighbour). The Christian who does not do this does not love.

Under what forms should this residue be utilised? Particularly as gifts, the placing of money and investments.

The gifts could be to organisations and movements which work for the relief of poverty and the needs of the poor. There are many such to-day.

The surplus money should be placed in the light of the Church's teaching that worldly wealth is for the common good [103] : such money can be invested in undertakings useful to the community but the object is not solely one of profit. The Church has a tradition on this point in her historic attitude to usury.

Investments might be for setting up or developing an enterprise to give work to the unemployed and thus would distribute the use of wealth for the benefit of all [104]. Always providing, says Pius XII, that such work should be directed to produce really useful goods... always serving the community [105]. Here the policy which creates false needs, through clever publicity, for the sake of large returns, must be condemned. On the same subject, what can be said of investments abroad made without any regard to the

(103) Pius XI, Quadragesimo Anno, "A man's surplus income is not left entirely to his own discretion".

(104) Father Bayart, "La propriété capitaliste et la doctrine sociale de l'Eglise". (Melange de Science religieuse, May and November, 1955, Lille).

(105) An important remark. St. Thomas explains why a law is recognised in all human necessities, which seems too strong to many: "That which belongs to human law should derogate the natural or divine law. Now, according to the natural order established by divine Providence, inferior beings are destined to provide for man's needs; their division and appropriation — the work of human law — cannot prevent them from providing the needs of man. This why whatever surplus wealth is held by some is due, by the natural law, to the sustenance of the poor". These and other texts show that social justice requires those who have surplus wealth to help those in need.

harmonious development of the country and which, in fact, upset its proper social and economic balance?

Second case: Case of extreme necessity. When a man finds himself in a state of extreme necessity there is a duty in justice to give him the necessities of life. One has no right to refuse them to him or to prevent him from taking them. On the contrary, he ought to take whatever is immediately necessary for him.

An example of what we mean is the present-day case of the *homeless* and of families which live in inhuman conditions in over-populated and insanitary dwellings. From this example one sees the actual meaning of the doctrine—the principle seemed remote and hypothetical. We are only beginning to see its practical implications. It is to be hoped that this social doctrine will begin to inspire our legislators to remedy, in the name of social justice, these disorders which are so obviously contrary to God's plan.

Third Principle : "The vital function of private ownership must be respected and protected in its personal and social role" (Pius XI) — *its legality.*

Private ownership has a vital function; it should serve personal, family and social life.

Personal life. Private ownership develops initiative and encourages men to make provision for the future. It is a stimulus to work and to save. It ensures the respect of man's dignity and freedom. That is why Pius XII links it to the freedom "from dependence and economic serfdom irreconcilable with human rights. Whether this serfdom comes from power of private capital or from the State the effect is the same" [106].

Family life. Ownership is necessary for family life to ensure its stability, cohesion, unity and independence. Pius XII defended the right of ownership in the name of the liberty of a father to provide

(106) Pope Pius XII, Christmas Message 1942.

for his family and fulfil his duties towards it [107]. He demands, for the family, vital living space.

Social life. Because — and this is a psychological statement of common sense and experience—man pays more attention to his own property than to that which does not belong to him, private ownership brings about better management of goods and society at large thus benefits. Furthermore, when it is exercised with the sense of its social function and the wise distribution of whatever is superfluous, it is the means wished for by God whereby, as the first principle laid down, the goods of creation attain their universal destination, being put to the service of all according to an order of justice and charity.

Fourth Principle: The present system of ownership is not unchangeable. It has undergone and will undergo further developments.

There is a fairly widespread opinion that the Church is bound to the present system of ownership. She is accused of not recognising the developments that the forms of ownership can undergo.

The whole social teaching of the Church refutes this very criticism. The Popes have lashed out against the weaknesses, anomalies and inequalities of the present system.

No. The Church is bound to no single system of ownership. The Church always defends the rights of the human person. She is as independent of all kinds of economic systems as she is of all political ones. Pius XI declared in Quadragesimo Anno : "History proves that ownership, like other elements of social life, is not absolutely rigid". The Pope then listed the various forms that ownership has taken; primitive forms of savage peoples, patriarchal era, feudal, monarchical and the varied forms of the modern age.

(107) Pope Pius XII, Message of 1st June, 1941.

CONCLUSIONS

1) The social teaching of the Church *bases the right to the use of material goods on the dignity of human person* for this dignity is superior to created things which have been placed by Providence at the disposal of all men. *The extension of private ownership to all* requires that the principle that material goods are destined for the use of all men should be practised according to justice and charity, as respected in human conventions.

2) *This doctrine establishes a synthesis between the personal and social role of ownership.* It calls on every Christian, and indeed on every man, to make this synthesis in his conscience and conduct. To sacrifice the first aspect is to fall into socialism or communism. Not to recognise the second is to return to liberalism and pagan concepts of ownership.

3) In the teaching of Pius XII a distinction between two forms of ownership emerges. On the one hand *personal and family ownership*, closely linked with the human person and, on the other, the larger forms of *capitalist ownership*. In both cases the Pope maintained the principle. But he vigorously denounced the abuses of the second category. It was in this sense that he condemned capitalism as "contrary to the natural law". "Wherever capitalism is based on false ideas and assumes a limitless right over its own property, without admitting any subordination to the common good, the Church has always condemned it as contrary to the natural law" [108].

It is true that the rapid development of economic structures seems opposed to the practice of the doctrine of personal and family ownership. The nature of the small family holding poses problems difficult to solve. First is that of change of residence to which the working population is subject owing to the "shifting of labour". Enquiries and census returns have shown how frequently this can occur to-day. Then there is the fact that the small house and garden lead to an agglomeration of such a size that the collective cost (roads, water, gas, electricity, sewage, transport, etc.) can-

[108] Pope Pius XII, Radio Message, 1st September, 1944.

not be met from municipal revenues. Finally, how can the small farmer stand up to the requirements and expense of the mechanisation of agriculture?

All these facts are indisputable and raise complicated problems. But first, as we have seen, the Popes agree that the Church cannot be bound to any one form of ownership. Their attitude with regard to developments in economic structure shows their independence in this sphere. Indeed it is here necessary to appeal to Christians "to find new forms of ownership which better correspond to the essential function of worldly goods, which is the flowering of human life in its individual and social aspects" [109].

On the other hand, in defending the right of ownership, the Pope places the metaphysical and moral point of view before everything else; the blossoming of the human person and the conditions of his freedom, responsibility and personal initiative remain essential whatever systems or forms prevail. The picture of the little house and garden does not show all the forms which family ownership can take in certain countries.

Finally, if the principle is abandoned, it must be seen that collectivism, with its grave consequences and problems, becomes the dominating power.

Second right : The right to work.

Popes Leo XIII and Pius XI both taught that work had a twofold character; it is both personal and necessary. Pius XII continued this teaching : [110] and completed it by developing a third characteristic : work is social.

First characteristic of work : it is personal.

The Principle : "It is personal" that is to say the worker's

---

(109) Mgr. Tiberghien: "Sens chrétien et vie social" p. 133.
(110) Pope Pius XII, Radio Message, 1st June, 1941: "It is personal because it is accomplished by uniquely human forces; it is necessary because without it the necessities of life cannot be procured".

human *person* in all its aspects is involved in his work. A person's entire physical resources, his faculties of intelligence, initiative, energy and will together with his responsibilities as a man and head of a family are involved. These, and his motives and attitude to work, should teach him the true meaning of work, which is : a means of earning his living so that he can lead a decent, human existence and raise and support a family. Work is the true expression of the human person.

The Applications : The applications of this principle proper to the doctrine of the Church, but which, nevertheless, everyone can and should accept, have been set out by the Popes.

First, on the *dignity of work*. Here again, the Church's social teaching is opposed both to Liberalism and Communism; to Liberalism, which equates work to merchandise, to Communism, which considers work solely as a productive force at the service of the Socialist State.

Both errors fail to recognise the personal character of work. They consider it as though it can be detached from the person of the worker, as though it were not inherent in his person. Socialism recognises the dignity of work but it puts this dignity into the work done and not in the person who does it.

For the Church's social doctrine, on the contrary, the dignity of work comes from the dignity of the human person of the worker. It is a *human* act. (Father Villain in "Enseignement social de l'Eglise", Vol. II, p. 62, says : "We are here at the antipodes of pure Socialist thought; for if man has dignity because he works his dignity is in his work and still more in the final product. We, on the contrary, say that it is man who gives work its dignity and that the source of the dignity of human work is in man".)

In the second place, the principle has its repercussions on the *conditions of work*. Because work is inseparable from the person and cannot be considered solely under its utilitarian and material aspects, the Popes have forcefully called for conditions of work which respect the personal character and dignity of the worker. These conditions should take into account the physical resources and limitations of man so that his body may not be crushed and his soul stifled : [111] Man must have time to relax and to observe the Sabbath. Allowance must be made for the age, sex and health of the worker and for the hazards inseparable from human life.

Finally, this principle is binding on the *State* which intervenes more and more in questions of the remuneration for work and which now itself owns certain industries. It should respect the personal character of work, says Pius XII, "both in principle and, as far as possible, in practice". Neither should the State's laws render impossible the other rights which the Pope listed [112].

The Second characteristic of work : It is *necessary* because it gives the worker the means of earning his living and providing for his family.

Principle : Every man has the duty, imposed by nature and his Creator, of preserving his existence which he holds from God. He has therefore the right—imposed by nature and not by society—of finding in his work the means of providing for himself and his children.

In this precise sense, we can speak of the right to work—the worker's natural right to accomplish his duty as a worker, "as the indispensable supporter of family life" (Pius XII). This does not mean, as some Socialists held in the 19th century, that every individual out of work has the right to demand employment from the State although, as we will see later, the State has the duty in certain cases to provide work. But it does mean that, in a well-organised society, every man has the right to find in his work whatever is necessary to live a human life.

Practical applications :

1) *For the remuneration of work; Wages:* The Church's social

---

(111) Leo XIII, Rerum Novarum: "To exercise pressure upon the indigent and the destitute for the sake of gain, and to gather one's profit out of the need of another, is condemned by all laws human and divine".

(112) Pope Pius XII, Radio Message, 1st June, 1941.

teaching has contributed greatly towards impressing on the public mind two essential ideas; the minimum living wage and the family wage [113].

The living wage.

The idea of a living wage is bound up with the essential character of work. Leo XIII in Rerum Novarum, fighting against the insufficiency of wages, then widespread under the free-trade system, taught that there was a minimum below which a wage would be unjust. This minimum is what is necessary for the workers subsistance. The Pope's text is well-known and had a great effect because he recalled the requirements of the moral law and justice : "Let the working-man and the employer make free agreements, and in particular let them agree freely as to the wages; nevertheless, there underlies a dictate of natural justice more imperious and ancient than any bargain between man and man, namely *that wages ought not to be insufficient to support a frugal and well-behaved wage earner.* If through necessity or fear of a worse evil the working-man accepts harder conditions because an employer or contractor will afford no better, he is made the victim of force and injustice". A wage is not just merely because it has been agreed upon between employer and worker for it can happen that the worker is not free to refuse because he must find work at any price. A wage is just if it is in conformity with the higher law of natural justice which recognises the *vital necessity* that the worker's wage should enable him to live as a human person.

In Quadragesimo Anno, Pius XI completed this idea of a living wage. He considered three factors in the remuneration for work. The first was *the needs of the worker.* He must keep himself and his family at a level which allows of a certain amount of leisure and ease and provides against natural risks of sickness and old age and occupational hazards. Then Pius XI also took into account the *situation of the business or industry and the requirements of the common good.* He called on social and vocational organisations for

(113) These two problems have caused years of discussion and study both on the part of theologians and sociologists.

F

a policy which would solve the problem of the living wage.

The social teaching of Pius XII is characterised by his insistence on a *just wage*. He came back time and time again to this point. He makes it, together with a better distribution of the natural goods, one of "the two most pressing requirements in the social programme of the Church" [114].

In the second place, the Pope undertakes *the defence of the women workers* and their wages : "the Church has always sustained the principle that, for the same work, the same salary should be paid—and women should be paid the same as men for the same work" [115]. The Pope denounces the injustice which can be done to the woman worker by workers themselves.

In the third place, a just wage, according to the Pope, is one which sustains the worker and *his family*. "It is that which ensures the existence of the family and which enables the parents to fulfil their natural right of raising a family which can be decently fed and clothed" [116].

The family wage :

The idea of the family wage is always intrinsically linked with that of the living wage. The Popes have laid down the principle. But they left professional and political men to find the technical solutions. Pius XI also paid tribute to those who found practical formulae, like that of family allowances, a system invented by a socially-minded Catholic, M. Romanet.

2)   Because work is necessary and a living wage is vital the Popes have called for a *proper organisation of the people's work*.

---

(114) Pope Pius XII, Radio Message, 11th March, 1951 to the Christian workers, technicians and managers of Spanish industry.

(115) Pope Pius XII, Allocution to members of the 1st Italian Congress of Women Workers, 15th August, 1945: "It is both unjust and contrary to the common good that a woman's work should be used only because it is cheaper, with bad results, not only for the women, but also for the male worker who is thus exposed to unemployment.

(116) Allocution to Italian workers, 13th June, 1943.

The right and duty of building this organisation belong to those who are most immediately concerned — employers and workers. One thus sees how organisation on vocational lines can meet the pressing needs of the social economy according to the ideas of the Popes.

In his message of 24th December, 1952, Pius XII declared :
"When private enterprise remains apathetic or insufficient, the public powers are obliged to procure employment in every way possible in undertaking works of public utility and to facilitate those looking for work by setting up Councils or Labour Exchanges". Where private enterprise fails the State must intervene and help in the distribution of work according to the requirements of the common good. Has not *the fight against unemployment* become one of the gravest preoccupations of the modern State? But the State is now too small a unit in this field. The problem is an international one. Pope Pius XII showed a most courageous attitude (see his Allocution of June 3rd, 1950, to an International Congress of Social Studies in Fribourg) calling for a coalition of the entire world, a universal collaboration of men of all nations to find the solutions together. It is not only a question of a better distribution of the total sum of the physical resources of all the workers of the world but of giving innumerable families sufficient scope to develop as natural, moral, legal and economic units. One can see how the Pope, here too, took the side of the family.

Third characteristic of work : it is social.

The idea is a noble one and is understood by militant Christians. It gives meaning to their work and provides an ideal for their social action.

The Church's social teaching considers work as the means offered by God to men to co-operate in His work of creation and build together an earthly kingdom.

Thus, Pope Pius XII revealed work as a unifying factor among men because of men's natures. It brings them together and links them in the accomplishment of an even greater task, that of procuring for society the goods and services which are necessary or useful for it [117]. It serves humanity and draws men nearer to God.

Furthermore, according to the Church's social teaching, work should become the means of human betterment. It tends to improve the moral and material well being of the worker and to develop his personality. Alas, the reality is usually far removed from this ideal. Work in factories, mines, and work-shops too often degrades and brutalises the human person. Pius XI said "Contrary to the plans of Providence, work, which was destined, even after Original Sin to perfect man materially and morally tends in such conditions to deprave him. Matter comes out ennobled from the work-shop while men are degraded and corrupted there" [118].

Here again we see the extent of the requirements of the Church's social teaching and the great changes she wants men to bring about so that society's organisation can come near to God's plan. "It is the complete and complex structure of society which needs to be changed and bettered" [119].

The high moral value of work. In God's plan work should help man to glorify God and sanctify himself. Even in the technological era the human person created by God and redeemed by Christ remains noble in himself and as a result his creative force and work have a more lasting worth. Thus consolidated, human work also has a high moral value and mankind at work constitutes a society which not only produces things but glorifies God. Man can therefore consider his work as an instrument of his own sanctification for in working he perfects the image of God in himself [120].

(117) Pope Pius XII, "Work unites men for the service of the people in a common effort which tends to the perfection of one and all to the glory of the Creator and of the Redeemer". Allocution to farmers, 16th November, 1946. Pope Pius XII, Letter to M. Charles Flory, 19th July, 1947. "In this sense, work is capable by its very nature, of closely uniting men together".

(118) Quadragesimo Anno.

(119) Pope Pius XII, Allocution to Italian workers, 13th June 1943.

(120) Pope Pius XII, Christmas Message, 1955.

Conclusion to Part One.

This concept of man that the Church's social teaching brings
to the modern world has certain characteristics that were underlined in the teachings and work of Pope Pius XII.

In the first place it is concerned with human interests. Far
from teaching a cold and inhuman doctrine Pius XII described
the sufferings and miseries of men in moving terms. Industrial and
agricultural workers, the unemployed and economically depressed,
the banished, exiles and migrants; children who have been abandoned, "families in blackest misery", the old and the poor; the
oppressed of all kinds, "all those who suffer affliction for any
reason", the millions haunted by the possibility of famine and the
under-nourished populations... the Pope thought of them all and
spoke of each group particularly. He explained that the sad chorus
came to him from all parts of the world and that "the sorrows and
tears it revealed rent his very heart" [121]. This is the echo of
Christ's cry of compassion and mercy which is prolonged to our
own day by His Vicar on earth : "I have had pity on the crowd"...
"My soul is sorrowful".

The Pope did not consider an abstract man, a "homo economicus", but living beings of flesh and blood who work, toil and
suffer. He saw people as human beings who loved, bore the responsibilities of a family, and had needs and aspirations which must
be taken into account in the name of justice and charity. We can
apply to Pius XII the words which he applied to the Church,
"Watching constantly over man, listening to his heart-beats she
knows his worth and perceives his aspirations with a clear sighted
intuition and that penetrating vision which can only come from
the supernatural light of the Church's doctrine and the supernatural warmth of His divine love" [122].

A second characteristic which cannot but strike those who too
lightly accuse the Church of not rating man highly enough, *is its
dynamic realism*. Man, wounded and weakened as he is by

(121) Radio Message, 24th December, 1952.
(122) Allocution to the Sacred College, 20th February, 1946.

Original Sin, is reminded by the Church that he still retains [123] the light of his intelligence and freedom and that he can and *must* fight if he is to be faithful to his supernatural duties and the natural law, and that he has the grace of God to help him. Pope Pius XII constantly and confidently called on man's freedom, will, energy and sense of responsibility so that he might take his place in the national economy and play an active role there instead of passively leaving everything to the State. The Pope required each man personally and all men together to participate in the formation of the new order. He proclaimed his "confidence in the sense of right and justice deeply anchored in the human person" [124].
This is true realism, "which determines, with the same certitude, the dignity of man and his limitations; his capacity to excel, but also the reality of sin", Pius XII, Christmas message, 1956.

In addition, how can one fail to be moved by the dignity of the interventions of the Pope as Head of the Church? He rose above the scramble of nations and all the powers of money, politics, governments, opinions and technical progress to *undertake the defence of man and call for the liberation of the human person.* The Pope defends man against the perils which menace him; against the errors and systems which belittle human nature and tend to drag man into the trap of false liberty, or enslave him to the dictatorship of a man or of a State. He also defends man against the abuses of economic systems, against the socialisation of everything, against the collective irresponsibility of impersonal owners and the hold of technocracy and against all outside pressures. The Pope warns man against the ambivalence of scientific progress and defends him in the spheres of medicine, psychoanalysis and surgery, as in the application of juridical sciences and the process of the law, including certain police methods.

For in the words of Pope Pius XII "everything should tend to the liberation of the human person. God has placed the human

(123) "Original sin and its consequences have deprived man, not of his power over the earth, but of his security in the service of that power." Pope Pius XII, Christmas Message, 1956.
(124) Pope Pius XII, Allocution to members of the International Institute for the unification of private law, 20th May, 1948.

person at the summit of the created universe, making him the
standard for everything in economics and politics" [125]

All inventions, progress, economics and techniques should be
judged in relation to man. "The Church's role is to establish here
an order of values and to subordinate factors of material progress
to pure spiritual elements" [126].

Finally, this concept of man regards him *as he is*. All branches
of knowledge—history, geography, sociology, psychology, law, the
sciences and medicine—should be devoted to the return to man,
the discovery of man and the search for the place which belongs
to him. In the midst of laborious efforts to get men to improve
international relations and find a true peace, Pope Pius XII, in his
Christmas Allocution of 1955, made an appeal which is a whole
programme in itself: "to refind peace and *give back to man his
place in the world*".

How could such a doctrine, taught fearlessly and with unflag-
ging perseverance, fail to have deep repercussions on the social
economy? This is what we will study in Part Two.

(125) Pope Pius XII, Letter of 14th July, 1945, to M. Charles Flory.
(126) Reply of Pope Pius XII to the Respects of the Diplomatic Corps
on his 80th birthday. (4th March, 1956).

PART TWO

THE CHRISTIAN CONCEPT
OF THE SOCIAL ECONOMY

The Church's social teaching gives our age a concept of social economy bound up with the Christian concept of man. There is a "Christian concept of the social economy" [127]. This second part will be devoted to its analysis. This concept shows us how, without intervening in the organisation of the technical aspects of the running of society, the Church fulfils her mission in the spiritual, moral and social order. She does not abandon men to their task but brings them the irreplaceable help of her principles, knowledge and experience of humanity, and the wisdom of her Popes, so that the citizens of this earthly kingdom and their governments can themselves build a social order nearer to the needs of men and leading to peace.

The Christian concept of the social economy can be recognised by the following characteristics. It is :

1) a *human* economy ;

2) an economy for the *common good* ;

3) an *organic* economy;

4) a *dynamic* economy inspired by the principles of charity and social justice;

5) finally, an economy obedient *to the moral law.*

(127) Pope Pius XII, to members of the World Congress of Chambers of Commerce, 27th April, 1950.

First Characteristic

A Human Economy

According to Pope Pius XII, the most important social problem is that of the organisation of a social economy which would be directed towards satisfying man's needs; an economy which would respect man's nature and dignity and provide the material conditions in which he can live as a man should.

There are several characteristic traits of such a human economy as described by the Popes :
1)   that it should be *at the service of man ;*
2)   that it should take into consideration *man's nature;*
3)   that it should adjust itself to *man's fundamental needs ;*
4)   that it should aim at *man's improvement ;*
5)   that it should be *available to all men ;*
6)   that it should *fit man* and be *made to a human scale.*

1)   *At man's service.*

The economy should respect, pursue and guarantee the *primacy* of man over all material things, whether wealth, production or technical progress. Man's proper place in society from which he has been debarred for too long must be restored to him [128]. It is possible to organise the economy without taking man into account so that a nation is considered only according to the riches and material wealth it has amassed. Everything must be sacrificed to production in such a society. The concept of a human economy entails a radical change from the ideas of the eighteenth and nineteenth century economists who used only natural philosophy, or from the concept of the totalitarian States which reduce everything to mere mechanics.

(128) Pope Pius XII, "The great wretchedness of the social order is that it is neither deeply Christian nor **truly human,** but purely technical and economic". Allocution to members of the Christian Union of the leaders of Italian industry, 31st January, 1952.

Not that a human concept of society fails to recognise the great importance of every nation's productivity, for without sufficient production there cannot be enough to go round [129] and the well-being of the population is sacrificed. But "productivity is not an end in itself" [130].

Furthermore, there is disruption when "this productivity is effected by means of unrestrained competition and the unscrupulous use of wealth or by despotic oppression and exploitation of labour and its particular needs, for the profit of State" [131]. The order which must be respected is that which puts man in the central place and puts economy at his service. The Church has consistently endeavoured to have man considered more important than economic and technical advantages [132].

2) *A human economy which takes into consideration human nature and the whole man.*

Technology is subordinate to man and to the sum of the spiritual and material values which concern his nature and personal dignity [133].

If man comes first it is because of the dignity of his human nature and person. The human economy is one which takes into account the complex nature, the living unity of body and soul, individuality and personality of the whole man, a spiritual and reasonable being, a free and social being, child of man and son of God [134].

---

(129) Pope Pius XII, Allocution to the Sacred College, 2nd June, 1948.
(130) Pope Pius XII, Discourse, 4th February, 1956, to representatives of business and trade unions.
(131) Pope Pius XII, Allocution to the Sacred College, 2nd June, 1948.
(132) Pope Pius XII, Radio Message, 11th March, 1951.
(133) Pope Pius XII, Christmas Radio Message, 1953.
(134) Pope Pius XII, "The Church has not kept a narrow concept of man because she knows the complexity of his nature and understands human nature better than others.
(Allocution to the International Federation of Engineers, 9th Oct., 1953).

—of man, the *corporal being,* needing food, health, relaxation and rest.

—of man, the *spiritual and rational being,* called to a life of reason and intelligence. A being called also to a spiritual, moral and religious life so that he may not remain a slave to his senses, whims, instincts, and passions but become "man" and realise his vocation as a human person — to recognise his dependence on God —finally, called to a life with God as His son. An economy which does not allow man to live this higher life is not a human economy.

— of man, *the social being,* bound to other men by a law of solidarity in the different societies where he lives and which are at the service of human person; particularly the family, his vocation, different sectors of life, the national and international community. A human economy is one which takes these social factors into account.

— of man, *the free being,* able to co-operate and unite with other men in the choice of means to guide the social economy to its true end [135]. A being free from centralised control of his economic and social life by rigid and mechanical formulae which, because they are so authoritarian and centralised, ignore all local and regional differences and do not sufficiently associate the members of the national community in the construction of the "City". All large scale plans are useful and necessary in so far as they serve man.

3)   A human economy is one which "should adjust itself to *man's fundamental needs"* [136].

In his message of 24th December, 1952, Pope Pius XII laid down the goal of the public economy in the following terms : "to ensure the permanent satisfaction of man's needs in goods and material services, directed in their turn to raising the moral, cultural and religious level".

(135) Pope Pius XII, Allocution of 7th March, 1948.
(136) Pope Pius XII, Allocution of 25th March, 1949, to the members of the International Labour Office.

An economy of *needs,* is one directed towards satisfying the "fundamental" needs of man; like food, clothing, housing, development of personality, education of children, healthy improvement of body and soul [137] and the real needs of man.

— thus, not an economy of *false needs,* artificially created by propaganda advertising.

— not an economy of *lucre,* for the profit of the capitalist financier who overshadows the economic scene and himself determines which needs shall be satisfied. These needs are expressed in terms of money and are founded on financial means and buying capacity and are thus for the people who have, leaving unsatisfied many of the needs of those who have not the resources to procure the necessities of life [137].

— not *an economy of luxury,* Pope Pius XII denounced at least twice (2nd November, 1950, and 8th March, 1952), "the intolerable growth of luxury spending, unnecessary and unreasonable spending which contrasts bitterly with the misery of many" [138].

— not a purely *quantative economy,* aiming above all at "an abundance of goods, their value calculated purely and simply on material standards" [139].

It is primarily a question of "relating production to consumption, wisely geared to the needs and dignity of man" [140].

---

(137) Pope Pius XII, "There are needs which must be satisfied immediately; food, clothing, housing, education of children and the true restoration of body and soul." (Allocution to the Catholic Association of Italian workers, 29th June, 1948).

(137) Pope Pius XII, "This is where the fundamental principles of economic liberalism also lead, **once the pursuit of lucre by financial capitalism** weighs down the economic life and **when the implications of the national economy are considered only from the point of view of their market-value".** Allocution to the International Congress on Rural Life, 2nd July, 1951.

(138) Pope Pius XII, Letter of 5th July, 1952, to M. Charles Flory.

(139) Pope Pius XII, Radio Message, 1st June, 1941.

(140) Pope Pius XII, Discourse of 3rd June, 1950, to the International Congress of Social Studies at the University of Fribourg.

One can see what the results of such principles would be. Production would no longer be solely for money and profit as it is in a capitalistic economy. It would no longer serve only the power, prestige and domination of the State as it does in the economy of the totalitarian State. Man would no longer be a mere robot or tool for production.

This is the perspective necessary to understand the severe judgment passed by Pius XII, following Pius XI, on liberal capitalism; "Thus", as our glorious predecessor Pius XI showed in his Encyclical Quadragesimo Anno, "it too often happens that *it is no longer human needs* which, according to their natural and objective importance, order the economic life and the use of capital, but, on the contrary, it is capital and its ambitions for gain which determine which needs will be satisfied and to what extent. *In such circumstances it is not human work in the service of the common good which attracts and uses capital but, on the contrary, capital which disposes at its pleasure of both man and his work, like bowls in the hand of the player"* [141].

4)   An economy which aims at improving, developing and perfecting human beings.

Pope Pius XII, speaking to the leaders of Italian industry at a Congress to study their mission in the economic reorganisation of the South of Italy, (a region particularly poverty-stricken), showed them the goal to be achieved; the end that individuals aim at, and to which the state as such is ordained, is the true improvement of a people and in consequence, the achievement of their lawful economic, social and cultural autonomy [142]. And thus the economy would be one of human progress, of "material prosperity for the whole population" [143], "a prosperity which in itself also constitutes a solid basis for cultural and religious life".

The economy would be for the worker's betterment because "the

(141) Pope Pius XII, Allocution to Italian farmers, 15th November, 1956.
(142) Pope Pius XII, Allocution of 6th June, 1955.
(143) Pope Pius XII, Discourse to Italian workers, 11th March, 1945.

working class, in that which concerns it, is called to-day to take on responsibilities it never knew in the past" [144].

Such a human economy would aim at raising the standard of living and the purchasing power of the workers and would also give the working class the chance to take its place, "its responsible part in the running of the national economy" [145], "with equal rights with regard to the other members" [146] and "access to the full exercise of its responsibilities" [147]. There is a duty to raise this class of men, who are exposed to economic hazards, to the level of other classes in society with defined rights [148].

Pius XII deplored the fact that workers should be as strangers in the economic life of the nation. They have the feeling that they are on the fringe of society. The Pope defended the principle that the working class should have a say in the management of economy. He based this view on the community of interest and responsibility between all those who take part in production. He wanted the workers to have a just and responsible part in the setting up and development of the social economy.

A fundamental point of the Church's social doctrine is the raising of man through the full development of all his faculties and attributes, spiritual and physical. This is the sacred and obligatory end of every social economy. It is the first of the essential rights of the human person which Pius XII listed. But Marx accused the Church of not wanting any improvement in the lives of the workers and of only preaching resignation and passive acceptance of their fate. What a horrible calumny, replied Pope Pius XII, who himself frequently demonstrated all that the Church had done and called for in the establishment of a more just social economy where the workers could, at last, live like human beings. It also often happens

(144) Pope Pius XII, Letter to Canon Cardjin, 21st March, 1949.

(145) Pope Pius XII, Discourse to Italian workers, 11th March, 1945.

(146) Pope Pius XII, Allocution to the 1st Italian Congress on Women workers, 15th August, 1945.

(147) Pope Pius XII, Discourse to the International Labour Organisation, November, 1954.

(148) Pope Pius XII, Radio Message to Austrian Catholics, 14th September, 1952.

that the Church's teaching on the duty of giving men the *"greatest possible spiritual and material well-being* in this life" [149] is ignored. The Church is accused of being disinterested in men's earthly welfare in her concern for their heavenly good. The Popes reply : Man was put into a social life so that, by fully cultivating his faculties to the glory of his Creator and faithfully fulfilling the duties of his profession or vocation, "he may ensure both his temporal and eternal happiness" [150]. Here is how Pius XII describes the social order at its best : "that all should be *subjects,* and lawfully participate in the formation of the social order and that all, following their art and their profession, can live peacefully and happily with sufficient means of existence......" [151].

5) A human economy is one which makes its benefits *available to all men.*

The end of the social economy is to "make available to all men, in a consistent fashion, the material conditions necessary for the development of their cultural and spiritual lives" [152].

Thus it cannot be an economy reserved for the privileged, nor for a financial oligarchy or for an economic dictatorship, as Pius XI pointed out in the third part of Quadragesimo Anno. Neither can it be an autarchical society, thinking only of its own people. It must be open to all in the spirit of international co-operation and friendliness for which Pius XII ceaselessly called [153].

6) A human economy should *fit man* and be *made to human scale.*

Is not this the preoccupation which alerted the Popes to the danger to the human person presented by impersonal and gigantic collective enterprises, either capitalist or socialist, in which man

---

(149) Pope Pius XI, Encyclical, Divini Illius Magistri.
(150) Pope Pius XI, Encyclical, Quadragesimo Anno.
(151) Pope Pius XII, Allocution, 12th September, 1948.
(152) Pope Pius XII, Allocution of 7th March, 1948, to the Congress on International Exchange.
(153) Pope Pius XII, particularly messages of 24th December, 1941 and 24th December, 1952.

G

disappears as a person and becomes nothing more than a cog in the huge machine ?   Of course the Pope recognised the marvellous results in these of the inventive and constructive power of the human mind. But he denounced the perils that may follow for man himself, the family and society.

Is it not the same anxiety which moved Pius XII to express his preference for the small or medium-sized enterprises where personal responsibility is directly involved and for an economy in which factories are more accessible to man, to his home, and less centralised?

Some will say; "a beautiful dream, but impracticable, the current is too strong and it carries all before it. Technical and productive processes require the centralisation of industry. The movement of history is towards centralisation in industry, finance and commerce."

It can be replied, first of all, that the Pope was conversant with the economic facts and knew well how to judge the situation *as it is*. His mission is to recall to men, in the name of the moral law, *what it ought to be* — at least the ideal — to which the requirements of humanity should be brought as close as possible.

But there is more to it than that. Who would dare to pretend that the progress of true civilisation, the material necessities of the people which require a nation to use its natural resources to the best advantage, a deeper realisation of the real wants of man, would not influence governments, economists, politicians and industrialists to look for other and more human solutions. Surely this is the inspiration which has already given rise to so many plans for the development of under-exploited areas, town-planning, investment, decentralisation, the location of industry and other projects of economic expansion? What may to-morrow bring if man succeeds in fully mastering atomic energy and automation [154].

(154) There has been a real, if small, movement towards decentralisation in France. There have been efforts to help industry in remote areas and to distribute factories and industries more rationally throughout the country — all of which has become possible with modern economic and industrial

So much so that, contrary to the theories which held good up to the War of 1940, an eminent French philosopher and social economist declared that "If France wants to develop the dynamism for balanced economic expansion she must turn her back on the industrial, financial and commercial expansion of the last century" (M. Charles Flory, at the opening of the Social Study Week in Marseilles, July, 1956).

The relevance of a human economy

If we wish to understand the relevance of the Church's social teaching it is sufficient to examine the present trends of economic science. Forty years ago students of political economy learned that it was the science of wealth, values and prices. A purely scientific concept prevailed, founded on a mechanical and physical analysis of economic phenomena.

To-day the efforts of eminent economists to understand the real needs of man and to integrate him into the study of economic mechanisms so that he becomes the centre of economic science, which, in turn, becomes the science of human activity, is both heartening and promising. It is enough to read the works of Henri Guitton [155], Francois Perroux [156], Andre Piettre [157] and Jean Marchal [158], to mention only professors in the State Universities. But, in justice, we must also mention the considerable influence exercised by the studies of Fr. Lebret and "Economie et humanisme", of "Action Populaire" with Fathers Desbuquois, Villain and Bigo, with the eminent professors of the Catholic Universities who all try to develop the Papal directives towards a more human economy.

techniques. The regions are being developed to the profit of the country as a whole.
(155) Henri Guitton, Professor in the Faculty of Law, Paris.
(156) Francois Perroux, Professor in the Faculty of Law, Paris.
(157) Andre Piettre. Professor in the Faculty of Law, Paris
(158) Marchal, Professor in the Faculty of Law, Paris.
Some English equivalents of the authors mentioned here would be Colin Clark, "Welfare and Taxation", (Catholic Social Guild, 1954); Alfred Marshall, "Principles of Economics" (Prentice Hall); Michael Fogarty, "Economic Control" (Routledge & Keegan Paul).

AN ECONOMY FOR THE COMMON GOOD

The doctrine of the common good is one of the fundamental bases of the social teaching of the Church. Originally it belonged solely to the Church's social teaching. Soon the value of its ideas captivated minds far removed from Catholicism. Statesmen took it as their inspiration and it was incorporated into currents of opinion and social ideas. Yet it is important not to allow the frequent misuse of the term, emptied of its moral connotations, to distort its true meaning.

Four points arise :

1) What is the common good?
2) What are its essential components?
3) Greatness of the common good.
4) Service of the common good and the State.

1.   WHAT IS THE COMMON GOOD ?

Pope Pius XII defined it as : to realise, in a lasting fashion and to *"preserve, develop and perfect the human person by facilitating the due fulfilment and realisation of the religious and cultural laws and values which the Creator has assigned to every man and to the human race* [159].

The word "good" has a special meaning in the social teaching of the Church. It is usually used in preference to the term "general *interest*". This latter indeed conjures up for many the idea of purely material and quantatitive advantages without taking quality into account. It has a connotation of egotistical gain and personal profit

(159) **Pope Pius XII, Radio Message,** 24th December, 1942.

without reference to whether they are honest or lawful. An example will illustrate this. How many people, purporting to invoke the general interest of the nation, do not hesitate to defend the entrepeneurs of the narcotics business and the shameful profiteers of the white slave traffic and public brothels, etc. Those who understand the general interest only in financial terms hold that it benefits the nation to let such enterprises flourish because they can yield taxes and special levies. In reality, such undertakings work only towards the nation's destruction.

Of course the common good is the lasting realisation of exterior conditions and it includes material things. But the name "good" has a moral significance and implies moral values. The "good" is that which perfects a human person...... that which perfects, achieves, and completes him as a rational and free human being...... that which provides the satisfaction not only of his material and physical needs but also of his noble aspirations as a man, the satisfaction of his intellectual, artistic, cultural and spiritual needs and thus provides peace, security, confidence and happiness.

Leo XIII set out the doctrine in these terms: "without any doubt the common good, whose acquisition should have the effect of *perfecting* men, is principally a moral good" [160].

The common good is defined in relation to man; it is the human good of a human community, whether family, professional, national or international. We will consider here the common good of the national community.

The common good is this human good, as we have defined it, applied to a human community. It is a general good, a good which is ensured by *general* outside conditions for *the general mass* of the people. It is a good which members of the national community should seek and bring about together because it answers the essential need of all human beings. All men are called to enjoy its benefits together because they are conferred on each man as a member of the social body. The common good requires the members

(160) Pope Leo XIII, Encyclical, Rerum Novarum.

of the national community to go beyond the particular or collective interests of political parties or professional or specialised groups so that they can establish conditions favourable to the life of the nation and to its prosperity, its greatness, its place in the community of nations and its mission in the service of mankind.

II. WHAT ARE THE ESSENTIAL COMPONENTS OF THE COMMON GOOD ?

A thorough study of papal teaching allows us to distinguish three essential components of the common good : 1) public order, 2) prosperity, 3) intellectual, spiritual and moral values.

1)   *A public and external order.*

Pope Pius XII, defining the end to which the social economy tends, (which is none other than the common good) declared : this end "is to make available in a stable manner, to all members of society, the necessary material conditions to develop their cultural and spiritual life". The Pope added; "Here, it is not possible to get any results without an *external order,* without the social norms which aim at obtaining this end and keeping it" [161].

The common good therefore presupposes a public, external order which would ensure protection of life and property, respect for freedoms and rights, defence of the country by land, sea and air and the exercise of justice by honest judges.

The Pope underlined the need for stability and permanence in the conditions of this public state. Nothing is more dangerous to the common good than upheavals, revolutions and crises in the government which has the responsibility for this public order.

The Pope also taught the necessity of having a *judicial status* to

(161) Discourse to members of the Congress on International Exchange, 7th March, 1948.

give this social life an external backing and protection and to guide the particular energies of all citizens in their co-operation for the common good. This public order would also afford a guarantee of security for all men [162].

2) *Material prosperity for the whole population.*

"The national economy, by its regular and peaceful development opens the way *to material prosperity for the whole population*" [163].

Earlier, Pope Leo XIII laid down the rôle of governments and the State in the encyclical Rerum Novarum "The foremost duty of the rulers of the State should be to make sure that the laws and institutions, the general character and administration of the commonwealth, shall be such as of themselves to realize *public well-being and private prosperity*".

What does this prosperity require ? First of all the material elements which the citizens can use in common or in which they share a sufficiency of produce, goods and commodities ...... easy communication by land, sea and air...... a prudent organisation of production to answer real needs, "the most balanced development of all the means of production over the whole territory inhabited by the same people" [164], the prosperity of industry, agriculture, commerce and trades......an equitable distribution of the national revenue between the different social groups, "a just and proper sharing by everyone in the wealth of the country......" [165], "an improvement in the standard of living of the different classes in the

---

(162) "In order that social life should attain the end wished for it by God it must have a judicial status as a help, refuge and protection, whose role it is to help and not dominate this social life and to develop and strengthen the vitality of society in the multiplicity of its objectives, directing individual energies in peaceful competition and defending them by all lawful and appropriate means against whatever would inhibit their full development". Radio Message, 1st June, 1941.

(163) Pope Pius XII, Discourse to Italian workers, 11th March, 1945.

(164) Pope Pius XII, Discourse to the International Congress on International Exchange, 7th March, 1948.

(165) Pope Pius XII, Discourse to Italian workers, 13th June, 1943.

nation and most particularly the popular masses, with an increase in their purchasing power for the most depressed sections......a clear, just and moderate fiscal policy.........financial equilibrium and a stable and strong currency which enjoys public confidence.

But the prosperity of a people lies not so much in these elements of the material, economic and social order as in fruitful, united families playing their part with others in life...... in its eager youth at work...... in an atmosphere of social peace and security, of loyal collaboration between the different professions for the common good [166], in a climate favourable to the flowering of intellectual, spiritual and moral values.

3) *Higher values of the intellectual, spiritual, moral and religious order.*

The common good of a nation calls on the combined forces of savants, inventors, thinkers, intellectuals, and scientists.

In the intellectual and moral order the common good of society demands general education, the development of intellectual, humanistic or technical training, culture and different forms of art. The common good requires that the souls, consciences, will and energies of young people should be developed to awaken in them a strong, balanced and disciplined personality. Youth must be trained to submit its whims and passions to a higher law, to practise virtue and give itself to a high and noble ideal. This whole work of integral education presupposes the love of the good, of the true and the beautiful and the struggle against egoism, laziness and cowardice.

The Popes recalled the primordial place and good influence of the moral virtues among the essential elements of the common good : loyalty, courage, honour, patriotism, professional ethics and the love of work. Pope Pius XII insisted on "a full, personal responsibility in the temporal order as well as in the eternal" [167].

(166) Pope Pius XI, Encyclical, Divini Illius Magistri.
(167) Radio Message, 24th December, 1942.

Speaking of social reforms "such as are urgently required by the necessities and desires of our times", the Pope declared that; "some require a spirit of renunciation and sacrifice, others a sense of responsibility and endurance and all call for hard and arduous work" [168].

Finally, the common good, as envisaged by the social teaching of the Church, puts respect for religion in the first place because of what it is, the homage rendered to God. It is the supreme good also by virtue of its influence on men's minds, their families and social contacts and the way in which it educates them in the meaning of the common good. Leo XIII wrote, "to procure the common good is to make religion esteemed above all else and to extend its influence, so natural and marvellously salutary, to political, domestic and economic interests" [169].

III. THE GREATNESS AND IMPORTANCE OF THE COMMON GOOD.

All the Popes have taught the importance, the necessity and the greatness of the common good. Leo XIII said of the common good "This good, is, after God, the first and last law in society" [170].

Pius XI showed how the common good was called for by the social nature of man and the end of society : "The true common good is determined and recognised, in the last analysis, by *the nature of man* which harmoniously balances personal rights *and social* duties and by *the end of society,* also determined by this same human nature...... To deviate from this order is to overthrow the pillars on which society rests and thus to jeopardise the tranquility, security and very existence of society" [171].

(168) Allocution to the Sacred College, 2nd June, 1948.
(169) Leo XIII, Encyclical, Permoti Nos.
(170) Leo XIII, "In the midst of cares," 16th February, 1892.
(171) Pius XI, Encyclical on Nazism, "Mit Brennender Sorge".

Pope Pius XII, who frequently defined the common good, taught that one of its essential principles was, "the *overriding requirement* of society to place the common good beyond personal advantage, the service of each for all" [172].

The greatness of the common good lies in the fact that it is in accordance with *God's plan* which united all men in a common nature and put them to live in society. Men were destined to make use of the conditions of their life in common to direct them towards the good and to pursue their destiny by helping each other.

The common good of society is great also because *the good which conditions the existence, vitality, well-being and happiness* of a people *is greater than* individual or particular goods, limited to their own sphere of families, professions or groups. It alone can realise the unity and greatness of a nation. It has a universal scope and effectiveness and applies not only within every section of society but also to the relations of the sections with each other.

Another aspect of the greatness of the common good is that its role is to "safeguard the intangible domain of the rights of the human person and to help him to fulfil his duties" [173]. It is great because it is addressed to man as a whole, to invite him to reach out to realise his destiny, to fulfil himself in helping others to become better, more free and human, to discipline his selfishness, to rise above his petty personal interests, to take his responsibilities in the social body and to practise all the virtues included in the giving of self to this higher ideal. Social justice animates all the virtues which make up the greatness of man and puts them at the service of the comon good [174].

The greatness of the common good lies in the fact that it is addressed *to all men,* to all families and all societies which are

(172) Pius XII, Allocution of 16th July, to the U.S. delegates to the International Labour Office.
(173) Pius XII, Message, 1st June, 1941.
(174) Pope Pius XI, "The Public institutions of the nations must be such as to make the whole of human society conform to the needs of the common good, that is, to the standard of social justice". (Quadragesimo Anno).

encouraged to emulate each other and to *co-ordinate all their efforts*. It has in itself a power to work wonderful changes in the life of a nation and to ensure its social rehabilitation.

The greatness of the common good is that, far from shutting a nation in on itself, it calls it to co-operate for the international common good and the good of all mankind.

Finally, since the supreme common good is God Himself, the search for the common good, prepares men to turn towards the Father of all who should Himself, after having been their most consistent good here on earth, be "a magnificent recompense" hereafter.

IV. THE SERVICE OF THE COMMON GOOD.

Because of its greatness and importance the common good should be sought, loved and served by all citizens. It is the object of this higher charity, of which Pius XI said; "such is the domain of the body politic which considers the interests of society as a whole and which on this account is the field of the most vast charity, of political charity, of which it can be said that no charity is greater except that of religion" [175].

The State. However, the service of the common good is primarily the proper mission of the State and of governments.

Leo XIII wrote : "considered in its nature, the civil power is set up to attend to the common good which is the supreme end that gives human society its origin" [176]. And again : "The civil authority should not, under any pretext, serve to the advantage of one or a few, because it was *constituted for the common good*" [177].

(175) Pius XI, Discourse to the Italian University Catholic Federation, 18th December, 1927.
(176) Leo XIII, "In the midst of cares," 16th February, 1892.
(177) Leo XIII, Immortale Dei, 1885.

Pope Pius XII declared that this was the soul of every State. "The intimate and profound sense of the common good is the soul of every State" [178]. All the activities of the State are pre-ordained to this end. "All economic and political activity of the State is ordered towards the lasting realisation of the common good" [179]. Better still : "This common good is *the end* and *the principle* of the State and of its organs" [180].

How can the State fulfil this mission towards the common good? By its laws and institutions and the services which stem from its government and administration. "The mission of the State is to control, help and regulate the private and individual activities of national life to make them converge harmoniously for the common good" [181].

The State should first of all "have equal care for all classes of her citizens strictly observing the laws of distributive justice" [182] and protecting the rights of one and all.

It ought nevertheless to realise that "the weak and poor have a claim to special consideration. The richer class have many ways of shielding themselves, and stand less in need of help from the State; whereas the mass of the poor have no resources of their own to fall back upon, and must chiefly depend upon the assistance of the State. And it is for this reason that wage-earners, since they mostly belong to that class, should be specially cared for and protected by the government" [182]. Leo XIII also taught the important position of the workers. "Justice, therefore, demands that the interests of the working-classes should be carefully watched over by the administration...... It follows that whatever shall appear to prove conducive to the well-being of those who work should obtain favourable consideration. There is no fear that solicitude of this kind will be

(178) Pope Pius XII, Radio Message to the Swiss people, 15th September, 1946.
(179) Pope Pius XII, Radio Message, 24th December, 1942.
(180) Pope Pius XII, Discourse to the Roman aristocracy, 8th Jan, 1947.
(181) Pope Pius XII, Encyclical, Summi Pontificatus.
(182) Leo XIII, Rerum Novarum.
(182) Pius XI, Quadragesimo Anno.

harmful to any interest : on the contrary, it will be to the advantage of all; for it cannot but be good for the commonwealth to shield from misery those on whom it so largely depends for the things that it needs" [183]. Thus it is the desire for the common good which imposes a particular duty on the State to protect the mass of workers by its laws.

In conclusion: Three remarks are useful here.

1. It is superfluous to underline the *relevance* and the urgent necessity of this chapter of the Church's social teaching. The main reason for the decadence of society is that to-day the common good is ignored, disowned, ridiculed and betrayed. There is a race for selfish pleasure and a coalition of private and corporate interests against the common good. "Every man for himself". "Get to the top by any means — but get there". Except for a small élite the great majority of men have lost the sense of service for the common good.

As we indicated at the beginning of this chapter there has been a lamentable confusion between two concepts. The spiritual concept of the common good has been too long eclipsed by the materialistic concept of the general interest. To talk of the general interest is to interpolate and add particular interests; meanness, selfishness hedonism and self-interest all enter in. In making known the idea of the common good the Popes' teaching has unmasked the false meaning.

2. Are we sufficiently aware of the considerable influence wielded by the Popes' interventions against liberalism and in favour of social legislation by the State, which brought just reforms into the workers' lives? Two dates should be noted. The Encyclical was in 1891 — but the first French labour law to protect women and children at work dates from 1892 and was initiated by a Catholic, de Mun.

In Quadragesimo Anno, Pius XI described the extraordinary

(183) Leo XIII, Rerum Novarum.

impression made by Rerum Novarum on statesmen, parliamentarians and on the masses themselves [184].

3.   There is not the same difficulty in getting public opinion to accept the State's intervention to-day. On the contrary, the danger lies in the opposite direction — excessive centralisation and a statism which jeopardises the rights of the human person. That is why Pius XII ranked the State's protection of these rights of the first importance : "To safeguard the intangible domain of the human person and to help him to fulfil his duties should be the primary role of all public power. Surely this is the true meaning of the common good that the State is called upon to promote" [185].

---

(184) "Nor was the Apostolic voice raised in vain. It was listened to with admiration ...... not only by the loyal children of the Church but ...by Christian working-men...... and by all those devoted men whose concern it had long been to better the conditions of labour". Pius XI, Quadragesimo Anno.

(185) Pope Pius XII, Radio Message, 1st June, 1941.

Third Characteristic

AN ORGANIC ECONOMY

1. — It is an *organic* economy, first in the sense that it should help to give society the *unity of an organism*. "The economy of a people is an organic whole; an organic whole in which all the productive possibilities of the national territory should be developed in a wise and balanced fashion" (Pius XII, 15-11-1946).

The Popes sought to inspire men to apply to the social body St. Paul's image of the unity of the physical body. As in the physical body the members work in the unity of the whole through the diversity of their functions. Thus the organic concept of the economy should seek the necessary unity of the social organism above and beyond diversities of work, professions and classes so that a single body is formed [186].

Nevertheless, as Pius XII specified, if the comparison with the physical body is useful as a starting point, it should be quickly outstripped when it is applied to the social community, because of the dignity of every human being. In the physical organism, the organs are integrated parts of the whole and have no meaning or end in themselves. The unity of the whole exists in itself even if an organ is lacking. In the community of men, on the contrary, each human person has his own dignity and his personal destiny. He is not merely an organ, an instrument, or a cog in the wheel. The members of the community form a *unity of purpose and action* in the sense that they are, by the wise use of their freedom and consciousness of their solidarity, co-operators and instruments for the achievement of the common good [187].

By this organic concept of the social economy, the Church's social teaching reacts on the one hand against the abuses of an

---

(186) Pope Pius XII, 31st January, 1952 and Allocution of 7th March, 1948, to the Congress on International Exchange.

(187) Pius XII, Allocution to the Congress on the histo-pathology of the nervous system, 14th September, 1952.

over-individualistic view of the liberal economy and, on the other, against an over-organised concept of society which can trample on the human person and man's conscience [188].

In considering the ideal of the unity of the moral community the Popes came up against and analysed the brutal fact of class-warfare. They have all described the deplorable results of this conflict which makes impossible the establishment of this unity of the body, which is necessary for life itself.

This is why the Church teaches that there is a *community of interests higher* than the diversity of functions and the different interests which naturally follow. There is a solidarity between all those, employers and workers, masters and servants, directors and staff, who work together in the same line of business. The Church sees between them "a higher unity...... to know their interdependence and common interest in their duty to work together consistently for the common good and the needs of the whole community". And Pius XII expressed the Church's will on this point : "This solidarity should extend to all branches of production and become the basis of *a better economic order*" [189]. The Pope saw "the foundation of the future social order" [190] in this higher unity between all those who contribute to production.

Objection.

Here we come across a widespread objection. "Class warfare exists. Indeed it is capitalism which provoked it. It is an historical fact. The only way for the working-class to put an end to the injustice with which it is victimised is to go right into the war against the capitalists. Appeals for understanding between the classes are sentimental illusions which benefit only those in possession".

Reply: 1.   It is true that class warfare exists between employers and workers and that it for too long reacted in favour of the wealthy.

---

(188) Pius XII, Radio Message, 24th December, 1952.
(189) Pope Pius XII, Allocution to Italian workers, 11th March, 1945.
(190) Pope Pius XII, Allocution of 25th January, 1946.

It is no less true that the working-class has had to fight for its freedoms and betterment by strikes which showed the strength of organised force.

Finally, it is certain that there will always be tensions between different classes and groups of human beings. Some of these are even beneficial. The problem is to reconcile them in terms of justice and the common good.

But war between nations is also a fact of all ages and nevertheless the Church has not resigned herself to it but has always desired and preached peace in justice and right. The system of wars is being gradually replaced by that of peaceful relations between nations and who will deny that this would represent an enormous step forward in human progress? Every substitution of right for force marks a victory for mankind. If this be the case why cannot this progress in international relations be extended to relations between the classes? "Class warfare should be overcome by the inauguration of an organic order uniting owners and workers" [191].

2. It would be wrong and confusing to suppose that the Church by her teaching calls for an end to the struggle for justice. The two things are quite different. Christians have no right to resign themselves to injustice. Pope Pius XII recalled [192] that the Church "always fought loyally to *defend the human rights of the workers*. Fought loyally — because the Church believed herself *obliged before God and by the law of Christ* to do so. Fought loyally — not to stir up class hatred but to guarantee the working-class a position as sure and lasting as that already enjoyed by other classes and ranks".

3. We must go further. Class warfare should be ended not just because the forces of each side so evenly balanced that they are stabilised in a sort of cold war but because all classes should *together fight for social justice* — which is the greatest good. *Each one should co-operate according to his means to bring it about* just as

(191) Pope Pius XII, Radio Message to Austrian Catholics, 14th September, 1952.
(192) Pope Pius XII, Allocution to the first Italian congress on women workers, 15th August 1945.

all nations should achieve peace together and co-operate in its establishment.

It has not been sufficiently noted that this union of the classes, constantly advocated and called for by the Popes, should come about *in view of an objective which is too great for any one of them to accomplish singly.* This objective is that of the common good and needs of the whole community [193]. This requires the help of employers and capitalists as well as of the workers. The surest way to block it and intensify the struggle is to consistently resist all reasonable demands for change. Furthermore, this common good is concerned not only with relations between two classes but also with the whole economic, social and political structure.

II. —   It is also an *organic* economy in the sense that it is based on *vocational organisation* in all branches of production. The importance of intermediary bodies between the State and the individual is a key idea in the Church's social teaching. These bodies are nearer to the true needs of man and are more easily able to make the best use of his personal initiative and responsibility. They keep the State from becoming top-heavy.

Leo XIII, in Rerum Novarum, affirmed the natural right of association and declared that the State should respect and protect the right of associations to govern themselves as long as they were not contrary to the common good. It was at the time a daring act for the Pope because public authorities had been for a long time refusing this right to workers' groups [194].

Nevertheless Leo XIII did not yet formalise a type of vocational organisation. He aimed at composite societies, either of workers only or of both workers and employers.

Pius XI, in Quadragesimo Anno, indicated a definite formula

---

(193) Pope Pius XII, Allocution, 25th January, 1946.
(194) In France, corporations were abolished in 1791. Workers only gained the right to strike in 1864 and had to wait until 1884 for the right to form trade unions.

" 'corporative' vocational organisation". It underlined the *evil* of the bitter war between the classes. The *remedy* as he saw it lay in basing the social life on vocational lines and not on distinctions of class. The *instrument* would be the organisation of vocational bodies which would be like the organs of society (if not *essential* and constitutional like the family or the civil society at least *natural* and in conformity with the needs of human nature). The *end* of this vocational organisation would be the search for the common good of the group and its direction to the common good of society.

Pope Pius XII took up the programme of vocational organisation and defined it. He underlined its importance in an Allocution of 1952 when he protested against those who applied certain extracts of his predecessor's Encyclical to themselves while they passed over in silence "the principal part of the Encyclical, Quadragesimo Anno, which contains this programme i.e. the idea of the corporative vocational order of the whole economy" [195].

What is important, said the Pope, is "to work in good faith and fervently for the realisation of the thing itself and its many practical applications".

Pius XII saw, in this reform, "a new grouping of the productive forces of the people" [196]....

----

[195] Allocution to members of the Christian Union of leaders of Italian Industry, 31st January, 1952. It is important to note that this word "corporative" has certain Fascist connotations for some people in France and Italy.

It is important therefore to remember that in Quadragesimo Anno, Pius XI, denounced the "excessively bureaucratic and political character" Mussolinis' corporative organisation and the fact that, notwithstanding its general advantages, "it ends in serving particular political aims rather than...a better social order" Pius XII later made it quite clear that there was no intention of attempting to return to the Middle Ages — which is another connotation of the word for some. Certainly the Popes never intended the word "corporative" to start controversies which might obscure the nature of the reforms which are necessary and indeed they more frequently use the word "vocational".

[196] Allocution to members of the Congress of the Christian Association of Italian Workers, 11th March, 1945.

In the Pope's teaching on this point it is useful to distinguish three closely linked problems : the trade union, the vocational organisation and the legal status of professional bodies.

I. *The Trade Unions.*

The Pope spoke frequently about them. He defined the aim, their raison d'etre and their legality.

Their primary aim is to "defend the worker's interests in labour agreements" [196].

Their raison d'etre is that "they arose as a spontaneous and necessary result of capitalism as an economic system" [197]. Their legality has been affirmed on numerous occasions by the Church. Speaking to Italian workers, Pius XII said : "In the Trade union as such you see a solid support for the economic society of our time which has been more than once recognised in the social teaching of the Church" [197].

The trade unions recognised as necessary by the Church are those which, while they defend the workers' rights and interests, try to overcome class-warfare by working towards a constructive programme which takes into account the general state of the economy. Under this heading they can be the natural basic organs of vocational organisation; different unions of owners, managers, technicians, workers and employees.

2. *The Vocational Organisation.*

Its *end* is to set up normal, regular and organic *links* between members of the same business so that they can all work together for the good of the vocational group and that of the whole community no matter how different their work or place within the group may be.

---

(197) Allocution to the Workers' Christian Movement of Belgium, 11th September, 1949.
(197) (again) Discourse to Italian Workers, 29th June, 1948.

Pius XII distinguished two planes on which members should come together : that of the profession or business and that of the national community.

The *common good of the profession or business* in which all the members are interested (workers, managers, directors, etc.) is that the profession or business should be stable and prosperous, that it should have good markets and outlets, that it should enable each of its members to lead a full human life and that their professional or business relations should be based on justice and loyal co-operation.

But many vocational groups consider only their own interest and advantage. This is one of the most striking signs of the present friction within the State. "Whether it is a question of employers' or workers' unions, of economic trusts or of professional or social groups (some of them even in the service of the State), these organisations have acquired a power which enables them to exert pressures on the government and the national life" [198].

That is why the Pope underlined the duty of every profession to co-operate for the *common good of the national community*. The Pope showed how workers and management in the same industry had a common interest in the national economy. "Management and workers are not irreconcilable antagonists. They are co-operators in a common task. They eat, so to speak, at the same table since they live, in the final analysis, from the net and gross profit of the national economy. Each gets his share as of right and on this account the one is not under an obligation to the other" [199]. They all have an interest in seeing that the table is well laden. The national economy is a communal table from which everyone should take his portion whether in the form of profits, wages or salary. Profits and wages, which seem in conflict within a single industry, are both part of the national income.

From this viewpoint the workers are on the same plane as their employers and this provides equality of rights and duties.

(198) Pope Pius XII, Letter of 14th July to the Social Week at Rennes.
(199) Pope Pius XII, Allocution to members of the International Union of Catholic Employers, 7th March, 1949.

Pius XII did not wish, any more than his predecessor, to pronounce on the *technical* problem of the structure of the vocational organization. The Popes feel that this is not a question within the Church's competence. Men can organise whatever forms appear best to them. They are free to lay down the rules and statutes most appropriate to the national temperament and the needs of each country! There is no single, rigid formula other than that justice and the common good of the society should be guaranteed. It is well known how socially minded Catholics have devised different machinery for vocational organisation — work committees, mixed commissions and collective work conventions. Pius XII himself enumerated the different aspects of such organisation in his Allocution of the 25th January, 1946 [200].

The Advantages of Vocational Organisation

No matter what form vocational organisation may take the Popes' teaching has illustrated the advantages it can confer.

First, thanks to vocational organisation and its institutions *social justice* becomes possible and more easily applied for it keeps in check the type of competition which operates against the true interests of the workers.

Furthermore, vocational organisation opens up to the workers the means of taking *their share of the responsibility* in the running of the national economy.

Finally, this great organisation of vocational bodies, establishing as it does organic links between capital and labour, prepares the way for internal peace and harmony.

3. *The legal structure of economic and social life organised on a professional basis.*

If we make the necessary adjustments we can apply here the rules which Pius XII assigned to the legal structure of society itself. "If social life, such as God wills it, is to attain its end it

(200) Allocution to owners and workers of the Italian electricity industry.

needs a legal structure for its *support, defence and protection*. The function of this structure is not to dominate but to serve" [201].

This text can help us to understand better what is meant by the legal structure of a profession; which is not to say that this public legal structure will make the professional organisation into an organism of the State. A law which recognises a private organism does not thereby make it into a public organism.

For the chaotic system of free competition, dominated by profit, or the conflict between opposing interests, we must substitute a rule of right, institutions officially acknowledged by the State, and a charter determining the powers and necessary means to ensure the mission of the professional organisation. It is essential that this legal structure should serve "as a support" to the profession to define its functions on the technical, social and economic plane [202]. to ensure its place in society and to provide it with the means of economic expansion. This structure must also serve as a "defence and protection" in giving the profession certain disciplinary powers with sanctions, either in interior disputes which always endanger the unity of the professional community, or in conflicts with other professions or, finally, in relations with public authorities so that the demands of the common good of both the profession and that of the national community may be met. Such a structure prevents the coalition of powerful interests, monopolies, trusts and cartels.

"The function of the structure is not to dominate but to serve" said Pius XII. The State should, by the official recognition of professional organisations, help those concerned to organise their own affairs and not take on the job itself. The State is not there to direct but to encourage and promote such initiatives by its social and economic policies.

Pius XII insisted on the distinction between *private and public rights* and drew some important consequences on the nature of enterprise that we will discuss later.

(201) Message of 24th December, 1942.
(202) Some private French groups have already worked out the precise role of different jobs in a vocational organisation.

But first of all we must consider the principles of the Pope's social teaching concerning relations between the State and private enterprise in view of the problem of production. It is a delicate question. It is easy to misrepresent the Holy Father's teaching if one or other point of the doctrine is omitted.

PLANNING

First Principle : *the Pope frequently affirmed and recalled the need to organise social life, and in particular, production. He strongly underlined the State's mission in this domain. He recognised the usefulness of planning under certain conditions.*

"A just control of production does not leave out of account the principle governing State intervention which was brought to light by our illustrious predecessor, Leo XIII, particularly under present conditions" [203].

In an Allocution to members of the Sacred College on the 2nd June, 1948, [204] the Pope reiterated the necessity for a *wise organisation of production.* He particularly noted two things : first, the conditions of the national economy and then the relations between the national economies and the world market.

"All social reform is bound up with the question of wise organisation of production. Relations between agriculture and industry in the different national economies and the relations of these with each other and the manner and degree to which each nation participates in the world market are all difficult problems which arise in a different form to-day from that of other ages. The rational solution of these problems depends on the productivity of each nation and, as a result, the well-being of the individual, for it is clear that where there is not sufficient production there cannot be sufficient to distribute".

(203) Pope Pius XII, Letter to M. Charles Flory, 19th July, 1947
(204) Pope Pius XII, Allocution to the Sacred College of Cardinals, 2nd June, 1948.

On the 5th July, 1952 the Pope defined the State's function in the field of production.

"First of all the duty of increasing production and *distributing it wisely according to man's needs and dignity poses, as a question of prime importance, the control of the productive sector of the economy.* Thus, (without substituting oppressive power for the lawful autonomy of private enterprise) *the State undeniably has a co-ordinating role which is all the more necessary under present social conditions.*

In particular, its help is needed to set up that *kind of political economy* which boosts the active *co-operation* of all and the growth of production which is the direct source of the national income" [250]

All these texts should not be forgotten or passed over when we examine the Pope's position with regard to legitimate planning. Speaking of "plans" Pius XII declared, "we freely recognise that, within just limits, they can be desirable and even necessary according to the circumstances" [206].

Second principle: Even as he underlined the State's role in the organisation of production the *Pope warned against the dangers of over-rigid planning and an inhuman technocracy.*

Some people are amazed by the Pope's reservations with regard to these "plans" whose usefulness and necessity he nevertheless recognised. He gave his reasons clearly.

First, *he feared the over-rigidity of plans* which did not take sufficient account of man, his rights and his personal and family needs.

"Human society is not a machine and it must not be made such, not even in the economic field...... Indeed modern society, which would plan and organise everything, being regarded as a machine,

---

(205) Pope Pius XII, Letter to M. Charles Flory for the Social Study Week at Dijon.

(206) Pope Pius XII, Allocution of 5th August, 1950, to the International Congress on Administration.

comes into conflict with something living and which therefore cannot be made subject to quantitative calculations. More precisely, it comes into conflict with those rights which by nature man exercises on his own and personal responsibility — that is, as the author of a new life of which he is always the custodian" [207].

The Pope then cites the problems of the birth-rate and emigration which cause a profound conflict between the system and man's conscience.

He adds :
"These examples suffice to show how an organisation inspired by cold calculation becomes the negation of life itself which it tries to confine within the narrow limits of fixed norms as though it were a mere statistical phenomenon".

The Pope vigorously denounces :
"The rigid incomprehension of a society inflexible in its measures, which it devises according to calculations like a machine, but crushes without pity".

That is why the Pope demands that purely organisational experts should not have the last word.
"Who can fail to see in these conditions, the damage that would result if the final word in the affairs of the State were left to purely organisational experts ?" [208].

Of course their rôle is an important one. It can show results, but under certain conditions.
"Their work can contribute particularly to resolving the serious and widespread problems which affect the world, on condition that they apply themselves to improving and strengthening true human values."

In the second place if the Pope expressed some fears on the subject of plans it *was in so far as they reflected a stranglehold of the State.*

(207) Pope Pius XII, Radio Message, Christmas, 1952.
(208) Pope Pius XII, Allocution of 5th August, 1950.

"Once more, what we reject *is the stranglehold of the State*" [209]

"In some countries the State *is becoming a gigantic administrative machine. It extends its influence over almost every phase of life.* It would bring under its administration the whole gamut of political, economic, social and intellectual life, from birth to death". The Pope then denounced the evil which afflicts modern man *"the despoiling of man's personality"* [210].

Finally, the Pope feared "the danger that the state might be dominated by economic forces to the detriment of the common good"[211] and the use by a totalitarian State of these plans.

Experience has proved the fears of the Pope to have been well-founded. Events in Soviet Russia have shown that the use of integral planning by a totalitarian State, hungry for economic power, can result in a cruel oppression of the individual. For Stalin the important thing was not the fulfilment of the essential needs of all men. Priority was given to those sectors of the economy which were best able to build up a collectivist economy. The experience of Russia and of Jugoslavia has established "the radical unsuitability (explicitly recognised in Jugoslavia since 1952) of a policy of state centralised and integrated planning as a means of answering the economic needs of the people. The myth of integral planning having been shaken, the search for more flexible formulae was greatly helped" [212] "...*Planning had been the work of a team of technocrats completely devoted to the political party in power.* The two points of view, that of men's needs and that of the building of a powerful collectivist economy are as radically and intrinsically different as are men's needs and the pursuit of the maximum profit".

Integral planning is therefore no solution for it is incompatible with the common good. Other formulae which are more flexible

(209) Pope Pius XII, Allocution of 5th August, 1950
(210) Pope Pius XII, Radio Message, Christmas, 1952.
(211) Pope Pius XII, Letter of 19th July, 1947, to M. Charles Flory for the Social Study Week in Paris.
(212) M. Gilbert Blardone at the Social Study Week in Marseilles, 1956.

and avoid the very dangers denounced by the Pope can and should be studied.

NATIONALISATION.

The same reasons lay behind the Pope's caution with regard to certain public and judicial forms of organisation of the national economy, particularly *state ownership and the nationalisation of industry.*

Not that he rejected them a priori. Like Pius XI he held that the Church allows them within certain just limitations and "it is rightly contended that *certain forms of property must be reserved to the State, since they carry with them a power too great to be left to private individuals without injury to the community at large*" [213].

But the Pope did not accept State ownership as the normal rule of the public organisation of the economy. This would be "a reversal of the right order of things; the mission of the public right is, in effect, to serve private right and not to absorb it".

In another discourse [214] Pius XII stated the cases in which nationalisation is permissable. "Cases in which it is truly called for by the common good as the only really effective way to remedy an abuse or to avoid wasting the productive resources of the country and to ensure the organic control of these same resources to direct them to the best economic advantages of the nation". Thus, it is permissable, on the one hand, to remedy the abuse of mismanagement which would waste resources indispensible to the nation. On the other hand it is permissable to ensure that the general interest should predominate in industries vital to the economic life of the nation.

Here again we find that marvellous balance which characterises all the Church's social teaching. She gives the State a place of pri-

(213) Encyclical, Quadragesimo Anno.
(214) Pope Pius XII, Allocution to Italian Workers, 11th March, 1945.

mary importance and considers it "as a moral organisation, founded on the moral order of the world" [215], "as one of the constituent elements of the natural law" [216]. But on the other hand she demands that this natural law should always inspire the State's laws and that the State should therefore always respect the rights and free initiative of individuals, families and groups.

Structural Reforms of Enterprise.

Finally, the principle of the distinction between private and public right is again involved by Pius XII in the problem of structural reform of enterprise.

The Pope demanded that these reforms should be studied with care and due regard for justice and equity. In the midst of the War he proclaimed his duty to be "to warn nations and their leaders that after these disasters they will *have to build an economic and social order more in accord with divine law and human dignity,* uniting the postulates of true justice and Christian principles in close unity and guaranteeing salvation, well-being and peace for all..." "How indeed, after such hard years of suffering, anguish and misery, should men not rightly expect *a profound improvement in their conditions of existence?* Hence, these *projects for reorganising the world of work, these perspectives of structural reforms, this development of concepts of ownership and enterprise,* sometimes envisaged in passionate haste and doctrinal confusion, but which, nevertheless, must be compared with the immutable norms of reason and faith, such as the Church teaches"[217].

Pope Pius XI stated three of these structural reforms in particular in Quadragesimo Anno: "Wage-earners and other employees participate in the ownership or the management, or in some way share in the profits". Pius XI mentioned them as examples without

(215) Pope Pius XII, Allocution of 5th August, 1950, to the Congress of Administration.
(216) Pope Pius XII, Allocution of 5th August, 1950, to the Congress of Administration.
(217) Letter to M. Charles Flory, 14th July, 1945, for the Social Study Week in Toulouse.

passing any judgement except to say that they had been tried in various ways "to the no small gain both of the wage-earners and of the employers".

Furthermore, in the same Encyclical, the Pope, after having denounced the error of "those who hold that the wage-contract is essentially unjust" added "Nevertheless, in the present state of human society, We deem it advisable that the wage-contract should, when possible, be modified somewhat by a contract of partnership".

This evolution was most carefully considered by Pius XI as his expressions "somewhat" and "when possible" indicate.

Pope Pius XII tackled the problem in his message of the 1st September, 1944. He made clear distinction between small and medium-sized undertakings on the one hand, whose private ownership should be guaranteed, and large undertakings on the other. The latter, in cases in which it should seem to be more beneficial, the Pope declared "should offer *the possibilty of modifying the wage-contract by a contract with society*".

In 1949, after exaggerated interpretations of the text of Pius XI, hot controversy broke out in Germany on the problem of co-partnership. Some went so far as to say that it was a natural right. Pius XII had to intervene to declare that the right of co-partnership in private enterprise is not a requirement of the natural law. And this is where he made the distinction between public and private rights.

Business enterprise does not "of its nature" come within the sphere of the State's right. The relations between the participants are therefore determined by commutative justice which governs the contracts. They are not determined "by the rules of distributive justice so that all indiscriminately—whether or not they are owners—have their right to their share of the property or at least to the profits of the enterprise" [218].

(218) Discourse of 7th May, 1949, to the International Union of Catholic Employers.

Enterprise depends on the legal order of economic life and thus on contract. Because of this the heads of large enterprises, (and we are still speaking of these), can incorporate the most varied forms of workers' participation, whether in profit-sharing, bonuses, management or partnership. And in certain cases, where the "overwhelming power of anonymous capital, if left to itself, would obviously harm the community" [219] the State can interfere to give labour the opportunity to have its say in the administration of the enterprise.

We should note that the Pope feared the incursion of organisations having no connection with the enterprise into the sphere of management and the transfer of means of production to capital-holding combines. The Pope was always anxious to safeguard personal responsibility without pronouncing on the techinical aspect of these reforms. He also laid down, in his concepts of man and of the social economy, principles which called for prudent, progressive and far-reaching reforms in the structure of industry. These reforms should tend to develop and respect the personality of the workers. They should give labour greater responsibility within industry. They should give workers a more human and intelligent interest in their work so that it would become less brutalising and more educational and the workers could use it as a means to their improvement in an economy which would, as a result, become more organic. It too often happens that the workers have the feeling of belonging to a separate world, that they are kept on the outside and that there is no place for them in the life of the national economy. It is therefore easy to see the strong appeal of the Pope's call for the accession of the working class to the full exercise of its responsibilities in the national economy.

CONCLUSION

The present position of the problem of vocational organisation

It must be recognised that for too long this programme has been

---

(219) Letter of Mgr. Montini, 21st September, 1952, to the Italian Social Study Week.

little more than a dead letter—a fine programme that was never used.

But there are certain new factors which make it justifiable to say that, now at last, vocational organisation has come into its own. *The first factor is the ever-growing development of collective conventions* which form the basis for vocational organisation. In France, after about ten years of direct control, particularly up to 1950, during which the State rationed out raw materials and controlled credit, collective agreements were signed in 1950-1952. The first to organise themselves were the industries which were in difficulty or were undergoing a crisis and, as a result, were more aware of the need to protect the industry as a whole, e.g. textiles, transport and banks. Finally the big steel and building enterprises came in. It should also be noted that these collective agreements also settled essential questions such as the improvement of working conditions and the co-operation between employers and employees. This movement has developed particularly since 1955. From the 1st February, 1951, to the end of 1956, 2,180 collective conventions and 4,700 wage agreements were signed. These included 85 national conventions, notably building, public services, textiles and chemical products.

The second factor is the ever-increasing interest which the large employers' or workers' organisations take in the study of vocational organisation. For a long time — from the workers' side — the Christian trade unions put forward concrete plans. What is new is the work of the French Centre of Christian Employers and of groups of technicians and of young employers who have come up with definite projects [220].

It seems that, after years of inability to envisage any real transformation of the present economic systems, the experts are at last tackling it.

The third factor is that Catholics have been pioneers in this

(220) These can be seen in the documentation of the French "Centre du Patronat Chrétien". There have been similar movements in other countries, mainly in Europe.

development. The working out of programmes and projects has been obviously inspired by Pontifical teaching on vocational organisation. If Christians would decide to embark enthusiastically and soon on this course their action would have considerable repercussions on social life and would revolutionise the economy. While there is still time they should learn the greatness and the urgency of the task which binds them under two headings : as citizens charged with the construction and improvement of the earthly city and as Christians called to bring the world more into line with God's plan, in the name of their faith and the demands of social justice and charity.

Fourth Characteristic

A DYNAMIC ECONOMY INSPIRED BY SOCIAL JUSTICE AND CHARITY

In the Encyclical, Quadragesimo Anno, Pius XI hailed those "who seek to restore society in the spirit of the Church, closely united in justice and charity". It is important to realise the new depth which this word "social" has in relation to individual justice and charity towards individuals [221]. Pope Pius XII, speaking to the leaders of Italian industry, told them : "You have an excellent opportunity to practise justice and charity because you can give them a social meaning" [222].

1. SOCIAL JUSTICE

We will consider its objective, its basis, its requirements, and what it covers.

1) *Its objective:*

It is the service of the common good. It is the duty, in justice, of each citizen to contribute to the common good of society. Social

---

(221) Note: The Church's teaching distinguishes between justice and charity. Justice is the moral virtue which calls us to render to every man that which is due to him. Failure to practise this virtue calls for restitution. Charity towards our neighbour is the theological virtue which calls on us to love and help our fellow-men because God wills it and because this is the way in which we can show our love for Him. Failure to practise this virtue is a violation of the Divine law and can only be pardoned by God Himself.

Charity does not supersede justice; it inspires and governs it. Indeed charity obliges us to be just. An employer who thinks he can compensate for injustice towards his employees by donations to charitable causes has not understood what it is to be a **Christian** employer.

(222) Pope Pius XII, Allocution of 6th June, 1955, to the Christian Union of leaders of Italian Industry.

justice is a "community" affair which concerns itself with the common good and willingness to be of service. "The whole of human society," said Pius XI, "must conform to the needs of the common good, that is, to the standard of social justice." [223].

Thus, social justice is a special virtue with its own objective. It is different from "commutative" and "distributive" justice. "Commutative" justice is that which primarily affects individuals in their contractual relations with each other according to the principle of fair exchange ("I give you so that you may give me"). "Distributive" justice primarily affects the community and governs its relations with its members according to the distribution of social advantages (honours, remuneration, privileges, and assistance, etc.) and to its calls on these members.

Theologians have long defined *legal* justice which is concerned with law, as the virtue which guides legislators to make laws in the interests of the common good and which also obliges citizens to obey such laws.

Social justice coincides with legal justice when it is manifest in social laws made by the State for the common good. But it is wider and more extensive than legal justice in so far as it aims at the creation of a social order which requires the co-operation not only of the legislator but of all citizens and institutions.

Social justice is concerned with the relations of citizens with the common good both in their duties and rights. It is invoked in two ways, i.e. the relation of the community to the citizens and vice versa. On the one hand it demands respect for the natural *rights* of the members of the community so that they may be able to fulfil their *duties,* and functions in society [224]. On the other hand it is the virtue which influences citizens to render to society that which they owe it so that society may be able to fulfil its mission towards the common good by giving everyone what he requires to develop his personality and fulfil his social function.

(223) Quadragesimo Anno.
(224) Pope Pius XI defined social justice in the Encyclical, Quadragesimo Anno.

2) *The basis of social justice.*

The elements of social justice are : the social nature of man, the organic concept of society and the social end of material goods.

The first element of social justice is in *the social nature of man* in the sense that the individual can live and develop fully only in a society which provides all that is necessary for the physical, intellectual and moral life of man. Now there are several social categories which are deprived in some degree of this natural right. It is towards these categories which are in need and which have the right to live in a more human manner that social justice should first of all be directed. The duty arises from the nature which all men share in common and from the responsibilities which all citizens share, as members of society, towards their fellow-members who are deprived of the *practical* use of their natural rights in society.

The second element is the *organic concept of society.* Society is not a conglomeration of individuals thrown together — it is a living body whose members should help each other so that all can effectively take part in the life of the human community.

The third element is *the social end of material goods,* so that they can serve the needs of all according to the principles of a more just distribution of wealth.

To sum up, what the Church demands by social justice is "a just and proper sharing by all in the wealth of the nation" [225]. "It is important to give everyone what he is entitled to and to bring back the distribution of the resources of this world to the norms of social justice" [226].

3.   *The requirements of social justice.*

These are expressed by the creation of a judicial and social order

(225) **Pope Pius XII, Whitsun 1943,** Discourse to workers on social problems.
(226) Quadragesimo Anno.

destined to replace the economic life under the law of a just and effective guiding principle [226]. Class-warfare or absolutely free competition or an economic dictatorship (all forces which have withdrawn from the moral law) cannot ensure a well-ordered economic system. *"More lofty and noble principles must therefore be sought in order to control this dictatorship sternly and uncompromisingly; to wit, social justice and social charity. To that end all the institutions of public and social life must be imbued with the spirit of justice, which must be truly operative, must build up a juridical and social order pervading the whole economic regimè* [227].

In the same way Pius XII demanded that we should *"fully cooperate in the advent of a public order which realises, to the greatest possible degree, a sound economy and social justice"* [228]. It is not a question of a few reforms here and there but of a complete transformation of society.

Social justice is very demanding in its requirements. It embraces all the other virtues to bring about its objective, which is the common good. The repercussions on the lives of individuals and of society would be enormous if everybody were to consider the common good instead of purely selfish interests, to develop a social sense and bear in mind the consequences of his actions on others. As an example, take the virtue of prudence; the driver of a car can practise it to save himself or avoid prosecution. How different would be his driving were he to apply prudence in the name of social justice and positively co-operate in the common good by respecting the rules of the road irrespective of the fear of a penalty?

Take another example; temperance. Everyone can deny himself certain alcoholic drinks to safeguard his personal health. It is quite another thing to consider alcoholism as a grave social evil and to fight against it in the name of social justice.

This could be continued for every virtue; by passing from an in-

(227) Pope Pius XI, Quadragesimo Anno.
(228) Pope Pius XII, Allocution to the Sacred College of Cardinals, 2nd June, 1947.

dividualistic to a community concept, which ensures the idea of social justice, we bring about results which are beneficial to all.

4.   *The scope of social justice.*

Social justice applies wherever there is a question of the common good. Its domain is universal.

In particular, social justice arises in relations between workers and the community as a whole to complete whatever is due to the worker in strict "commutative" justice by the employer. Problems of family allowances, social insurance, protection and insurance against accidents, unemployment, sickness, disability, old age (homes and pensions) and, in a general way, vocational organisation and collective agreements should all be resolved and balance maintained between wages and prices.

Social justice requires the setting up of institutions and organisations which will allow workers and citizens to bring about reforms which would be beyond them as individuals.

Social justice overflows the national framework more and more, and now extends to relations between nations. It imposes on them the duty of co-operating to solve social problems. That is why Pius XII demanded, as we saw earlier, the universal co-operation of peoples and states to remedy the evil of unemployment. Each should bring its contribution according to its resources of raw materials, capital and man-power [229]. Social justice applies to the use of the different resources of the world.

(229) Pope Pius XII, Allocution of 3rd June, 1950, to the International Congress of Social Studies at the University of Fribourg.

II. SOCIAL CHARITY

After showing the necessity of the order of social justice Pius XI continued in Quadragesimo Anno : "Social charity should be as it were, the soul of this order, an order which the State must actively defend and vindicate". Too many Christians still do not know that charity is thus presented to them in a new dimension and that individual charity no longer suffices. There must be a *social* charity concerned with people but not just as separate individuals.

This virtue, still little studied by theologians and too little known by Christians on the whole, possesses a particular effectiveness in promoting social progress and in transforming temporal institutions. It inspires specialised Catholic Action to press its members to relieve the social tension between the classes and to change living conditions, outlook and customs and, indirectly, institutions. Thus the whole environment makes it possible to live a Christian life worthy of a son of God, and, opening to the redeeming grace of Jesus Christ and the Church's mediation, it directs itself towards the ideal of the restoration of all things in Christ.

Charity which concerns itself with the common good.

Like social justice, by which it is inspired, social charity disposes men to seek together the common good of society but its influence goes further into the very hearts of men. It first of all gives Christians new motives for social action, then a new objective for such action and, finally, the inspiration of a new principle.

a) *new motives:* These actions concerned with the common good are brought about by social charity and no longer in the name of the claims of justice nor under the compulsion of a rigid State law but *through love* — love of God and men. Men are no longer considered individually but are united in *society,* living in *a social body.* Social charity applies to life in a community.

b) *a new objective.* This temporal common good is pursued by social charity so that it may be directed to the *eternal good* and *destiny of man.* In other words social charity seeks a social order more in conformity with God's plan, more worthy of mankind redeemed and better able to ensure the human and supernatural fruition of the Redemption. It tries to bring about here on earth, an order of social relations between men which will prefigure the eternal city where all men will love each other in God.

c) *a new principle*. This principle *is divine*. It is that of the divine life of charity and grace which springs from the Heart of Jesus Christ, Head of the Mystical Body, and which is spread to the members of that Body the Holy Spirit, the soul of the Church. Through this life and all the virtues it enkindles, the Church, which is the Mystical Body, inspires mankind. It is by the Church's mediation that the fruitfulness of this life is transferred to the social body and it is through the conscience of the complete man (formed by her) that the Church ceaselessly works to establish the solid foundations of society.

"Considered from this point of view, one can say that the Church is the society of those who, under the supernatural influence of grace, in the perfection of their personal dignity as sons of God and in the harmonious development of all human dispositions and energies, build the powerful framework of the human community" [230].

We can call it a dynamic economy in the sense that the vital principles of social justice and charity are constant stimulants to combat stagnation, laissez-faire and conservatism hardened into the acceptance and maintenance of a state of social injustice. They press lay Christians, who follow the logic of their faith, to continually look for social progress and human betterment. These virtues impose a duty to refuse to be part of a social system which is contrary to God's will for the development of men and the organisation of society in justice and charity.

[230] Pope Pius XII, Allocution to the Consistory, 20th February, 1946.

Fifth Characteristic

AN ECONOMY SUBORDINATE TO THE MORAL LAW

The fifth characteristic of the social economy gives Christian thought a particular slant which makes it different from other concepts of the economy; it is the synthesis of the preceding characteristic.

The Church's social teaching does not accept the modern widespread thesis that the economy is outside the moral law. Of course the economy has its own laws and methods. The two domains are distinct but not separate. For, says Pius XII, "complete separation has no meaning in life, which is always a synthesis, since the sole subject of all kind of activity is the same man whose free and conscious actions cannot escape the moral law" [231].

The subject concerned in the economy is man and not the *homo economicus* which economic schools have built up out of an abstract idea; it is the whole man, of flesh and blood, the human person with his freedom and conscience, who is subject to the moral law in all that he does. It must be added that it is also man, the sinner, with his concupiscence, egoism and greed. This being so "theoretical autonomism as regards the moral law becomes, in fact, rebellion against the moral law" [232].

This is so true that the releasing of the economy from the moral law since the beginning of Liberalism in the last century down to our own day has resulted in a materialistic and soulless technical civilisation. It has caused terrible suffering and cruel anomalies.

We want to underline two aspects of the problem :
1) The Principle of the subordination of the economy to the moral law enlightens the judgement which Christians should make on

(231) Pope Pius XII, Message on the Family, 23rd March, 1952.
(232) Pope Pius XII, Message on the Family, 23rd March, 1952.

the different economies of capitalistic liberalism and Marxist communism.

2) The final solution of economic problems is found not only in the transformation of institutions but in the restoration of the moral law.

JUDGEMENT ON DIFFERENT ECONOMIES NOT IN ACCORD WITH THE MORAL LAW

It would be quite impossible to pass judgement on every type of economy so we will select two principal ones : liberal capitalism and Marxist communism [233]. The judgement of the Church's social teaching is concerned only with their disregard for the moral law. This affords the means of showing why the social teaching lays such stress on the subordination of the economy to the moral law.

1. — *Economic Liberalism*

Economic liberalism ignores and breaks the moral law in several ways :

1) in its *aim*. According to economic liberalism the most important aim of the economy is to produce more and more in order to have the greatest possible wealth and material prosperity.

Naturally the Church's social teaching does not underestimate the necessity for increased productivity as a condition for the temporal common good. But it also teaches that there is a hierarchy of values. The supreme value here below is neither the economic life nor material prosperity. It is man himself. Everything else should be subordinate to him, including economic life.

---

(233) We choose these two systems because they have been integrally applied and their principles are clear-cut.
As regards socialism, we consider Marxist socialism on the Marxist principles on which it is based. But there are many kinds of socialism and it is impossible to make a study of each type here.

Liberalism essentially has a concept of man and the social economy which is in conflict with this Christian concept.

2) in the *motivation* of economic activity — for liberalism — personal interest is the rule. Let everyone follow his own interests in perfect freedom and the general interest will be realised!

The Church's social teaching allows personal interest, profit and the honest growth of individual and family property. She sees them as a stimulus to man to fulfil his duty, as necessary for economic progress and as a return for services rendered. But the Church knows man and his deeply-rooted selfishness, the fruit of original sin; she knows that his passions are an obstacle to clear vision and the pursuit of the common good. She teaches that the common good will not be assured by giving full rein to individual freedom but that the moral law, which calls for justice and charity, must be obeyed.

3) in the *composition* of economic life; liberalism demands the complete liberty of the producer and free competition for the maximum profit. Thus, there is no room for economic and social groups such as vocational organisations or unions, which would limit or curtail the liberty of individuals.

Results. The door is open to all kinds of abuses in the exploitation of the worker.

Individualism is unleashed in business relations and bitter trade war, totally disregarding justice and charity, ensues between competitors.

Mammon is worshipped, the common good is systematically ignored and human values and God's plan are contradicted.

Such habitual conduct dulls the conscience. The producers, slaves of liberalism, become hard and insensitive to the sufferings and misery of men.

Finally, it makes the economy materialistic and pagan — the very opposite to the Christian concept of the social economy.

Liberal Capitalism.

The results mentioned above show why the Popes condemned liberal capitalism so severely.

Leo XIII — end of nineteenth century (1891) — This was the era of free competition. The pursuit of the maximum profit led the heads of industry to cut their prices and thus lower the conditions of the workers in order to beat their competitors.

In the encyclical, *Rerum Novarum,* Leo XIII denounced the low wages which the isolated and defenceless workers had to accept "at the mercy of inhuman masters and the greed of unbridled competition". The Pope also condemned the abuses in the working conditions of women and children who were hired because they could be paid less. Finally, the Pope denounced the overlong working hours and the absence of decent facilities and a weekly day of rest.

This amoral system which caused so many evils, was defined by Leo XIII by this striking contrast : on one side a concentration of wealth and the means of production in the hands of a few, and, on the other, the mass of the proletariat in poverty and under an almost servile yoke.

Pius XI — Forty years later. The liberal era was followed by an era of supercapitalism, "a veritable economic dictatorship" as the Pope called it in the Encyclical, Quadragesimo Anno. This is the age of big deals and mergers, cartels and trusts. "In our days not only wealth is accumulated, but immense power and despotic economic domination are concentrated in the hands of a few, who for the most part are not the owners, but only the trustees and directors of invested funds, which they administer at their own good pleasure".

Pius XI forcefully condemned the economic and social disorders of such a system and its inhuman character. *The whole economic life had become terribly hard, implacable and cruel.* There was "an unquenchable thirst for riches. . . ." "hardened against the stings of conscience". Many have been impelled *"to break the law of God and trample on the rights of their neighbour"*.

But what is the cause of these disorders? They are due to the *alienation of economic science from the moral law* [234].

Considered in the abstract this capitalist system is not bad in itself, declared Pius XI, but it has been vitiated. *"But it violates right order whenever capital employs the worker or the proletariat with a view and on such terms as to direct business and economic activity entirely at its own arbitrary will and its own advantage, without any regard to the human dignity of the workers, the social character of the economic règime, social justice and the common good".*

In 1937, in the Encyclical, Divini Redemptoris, where he states that "liberalism opened up the way for Communism", Pius XI condensed all his teaching of Quadragesimo Anno. He has "shown the means of saving the modern world from the misery into which amoral liberalism has plunged us". He adds, in addressing the employers, that they carry "the heavy inheritance of an *unjust economic system which has carried on its ravages throughout several generations".*

Naturally the Church's enemies continue to accuse her of never denouncing the economic system of liberal capitalism and even of being subject to it. The Popes indignantly refuted this accusation which they called a "calumny". A calumny indeed since the texts are there, clear, explicit and indisputable. What is true, unfortunately, is that too many leaders of industry chose to ignore them. Pius XI condemned this attitude severely.

Pius XII. We have already quoted from the great war-time messages of Pius XII — that of Christmas, 1942, condemning a social system opposed to God's order (see page 26) and that of September, 1944, condemning, as contrary to the natural law, a system which ar-

---

(234) Pope Pius XI, Quadragesimo Anno: "For at the time when the new economic order was beginning, the doctrines of rationalism had already taken firm hold of large numbers, and an economic science alien to the moral law quickly arose, and consequently free rein was given to man's inordinate desires.

rogates to itself an unlimited right of ownership without any reference to the common good. (see page 74).

Finally, in his Discourse for the Tenth Anniversary of the Christian Association of Italian Workers 1st May, 1955, Pius XII energetically protested against "the atrocious calumny that 'the Church is allied to capitalism against the workers' " and the Pope recalled his Christmas Message of 1942.

To sum up, the Church's social teaching, judging the capitalist system with reference to the moral law, condemns it not in its nature (for it recognises the lawfulness of income and profit once justice is respected), but for what it in fact does and practises. It is not only particular abuses and errors that are condemned but the *"social system"* itself where it is based on a concept of private ownership opposed to the community end assigned by God to the goods of the earth. Such a concept would ignore the common good and condemn the worker "to a dependence, to an economic servitude irreconcilable with the rights of the person" [235] and become "a power directed to the exploitation of the work of others" [236].

II — *Communism*

The Church's social teaching condemns communism for different reasons :

1) Because it is essentially *materialistic, atheistic and anti- Christian.* The concept it presents of man, life and society is contrary to Christian truth. The true destiny of man is ignored. Marxist Communism considers everything as depending on matter. For it neither the soul, nor God, exist. Society is considered as being created only for material prosperity. Communism denies that man's life has any sacred or spiritual character [237].

Communism sees religion as an obstacle to the liberation of man. Marx wanted a liberation which would not only free man socially

(235) Christmas Message, 1942.
(236) Christmas Message, 1941.
(237) Pope Pius XI, Encyclical, Divini Redemptoris.

from capitalism but also, spiritually, from God and religion. For him religion was the cause of fundamental alienation of man. (Marx considered that religion directed man from his vital rôle in the dialectic and thus distorted his true mission).

Communism has always and everywhere fought against religion and organised violent persecutions against the Church in the countries where it is master.

2) Because Communism ignores the *rights of the human person* and his dignity and freedom. It delivers him defenceless to the Communist State in absolute submission in the name of an inhuman totalitarianism which makes man a slave to production. That is why Pius XII can say that he condemned communism as *a social system because of Christian teaching.*

3) Because it *refuses to submit to a higher authority* than that of the individual, — to the authority of the moral law, natural right and God, the Sovereign Creator, Lawgiver and Judge.

4) Because it preaches *class-warfare* as an inescapable law of history and a duty which binds the workers, in violation of the law of universal charity.

Experience now shows how right the Church was to use these reasons, of a doctrinal nature, to denounce the dangers of Communism.

Communism was applied in Soviet Russia under Stalin's dictatorship. It is not a question of just a brief interlude for Stalin was head of the Party and of the country for thirty years. Neither is it a question of stories invented by the enemies of Communism for these revelations were made by Khrushchev himself, as Secretary General of the Communist Party, at the Twentieth Congress of the Communist Party of the Soviet Union, 25th February, 1956, in a supposedly confidential report [239].

(238) Pope Pius XII, Christmas Message, 1955.
(239) The report ends with these words: "No word of this matter should leak to the outside world; the press particularly should not be informed.

What then do we learn from this document? It described in sobering terms the implacable dictatorship which Stalin wielded over Soviet Russia, particularly since 1929 until his death.

Massive repressions were carried out by government machinery. There were numerous arrests of officials of the party, of the Soviets, and the army, often on warrants of arrest issued by Stalin himself in his arbitrary power, equipped with all the trappings of law and falsified documents [240]. "Physical pressure and torture" were applied "to deprive the accused of his faculties and judgement and take away his human dignity. That is how the 'confessions' were obtained" [241].

Then there were the mass deportations of many millions of people, "entire populations" says the report, and executions without trial.

The Communists, embarrassed by these revelations about facts which they would have preferred kept secret, tried, not to justify them, because they knew they could not, but to discount this testimony by declaring that, even if Stalin had committed certain "errors", he had also rendered immense services to the working-class and established great industries in his country for the material good of the people.

No-one can deny that there has been progress in Russia in the technical and material sectors of the national economy. We are only dealing here with the moral plane and it must therefore be stated that Stalin not only committed "errors" but veritable *crimes* which this report even severely condemns. But there is more to it than that and the lesson is surely that if Stalin committed so many

That is why we are considering it here, in secret session. There is a limit to everything and there is no reason why we should furnish our enemies with ammunition. There is no need to wash dirty linen in public." But the report was divulged.

(240) The doctors' plot, says the report, was "a pure invention from beginning to end".

(241) This part of the report confirms the judgement of world opinion on those who obtained false confessions from unfortunate victims, not only in Russia but in other countries subject to her yoke.

crimes over such a long period it is precisely because he deliberately ignored and openly violated all the rules of a universal moral law greater than the economy. *He did not recognise any authority other than himself — no moral law, no natural right, nor God.* He was the absolute master and, says the report, he made of himself "a superman, endowed with supernatural (sic) powers, equal to God".

Here an objection is offered : "but then the very interest of the party to which he was sincerely attached should have sufficed to stop him in his path".

The manner of the reply in the report is yet more striking. "In acting as he did, Stalin was *convinced that he acted in the interests of the working-class, in the interests of the people, for the victory of socialism and of communism"* — and the report ended on this note : *"This is where the tragedy lies."*

This is indeed where the tragedy of Communist morality lies. *According to it an act is not judged good because it conforms to an objective moral law; it is judged good because it is in the interests of the Party and of Communism.* Stalin logically applied the principle of Communist morality — once he felt he was acting in the interests of the Party and for the victory of Socialism there was nothing to make him pause in his criminal work. Here indeed the end was held to justify the means.

Would collective direction have prevented such folly? In collective or personal dictatorship the danger is the same once the party interest is placed above all moral rules. For since Stalin has died the interest of the Party has sent military divisions and tanks to massacre the populations of Berlin, Poznan and Budapest and the collective administration did not even demur.

There remains a final moral lesson to be gained from the experience of Stalin. According to Communism man is not the source of evil — this comes only from the structures of capitalism. As soon as these have been destroyed the Communist will make a "new man" and a true humanism will be possible.

We can study this claim in relation to Stalin's règime which

J

took place under unique conditions. Starting from a certain period when he had liquidated all his opponents and consolidated his Party [242] he was the uncontested head of Communism in his country. He was the arbiter of doctrine, of orthodoxy. By his position and temperament he was free from the slightest "pernicious" influence of the capitalist system.

But what does the report show? A man who was excessively brutal, capricious, autocratic in the extreme and who demanded absolute submission under pain of moral and physical annihilation and who was distrustful and unhealthily suspicious. After the war his mania for persecution reached unbelievable proportions. Fired with limitless vanity he re-wrote eulogies in his honour to attribute everyone else's achievements and genius to himself. He raised statues to himself when alive. Convinced that he never made a mistake he supposed himself to be infallible, knowing everything and capable of doing everything.

If we mention these traits of Stalin in the terms of the report it is because we touch here on one of the most irredeemable weaknesses of Communism. Since it denies the existence of evil in man's sin it is powerless to achieve the true remedy for such evil ... Of course economic structures have a powerful influence on man's social condition and we have already analysed the structures of the capitalist system in its serious attacks on the human person. But even if the structures of society were changed, as long as man keeps his sin, pride, ambition, jealousy and egoism there will be neither peace nor true happiness on earth. Doubtless Communism can inspire generous and even heroic sacrifices in its convinced militants for a certain time. But it is powerless to purify and liberate man from his evil tendencies, selfish instincts and the slavery of his passions. For that a redeemer is needed.

Stalin's conduct proved that, even in the highest position in the Party, there remains sinful man and in order to overcome himself he needs a morality which is greater than himself.

(242) "Stalin had recourse to extreme methods and massive oppressions even when the Revolution had succeeded, when the Soviet State had been consolidated and when the exploiters had been liquidated. . . ." (Report).

II

REFORMS IN PRACTICE

The Church's social doctrine teaches that it is not sufficient to transform the structures of society — it is necessary to have reform in practice.

Revolution, reform or transformation?

Here the question is raised : "Is the Church for or against the social revolution? If she is against it, will she be satisfied with mere reforms?"

The Church's social teaching has never favoured the social revolution for several reasons :

First of all this term "social revolution" implies violent disruptions, serious and unjust attacks on people and property, the kindling of passion and hatred, and the accumulation of disorder and ruin which remain for years.

Furthermore, those who have the revolution as their objective are inclined to "reject with understandable, but unreasonable and unjustifiable impatience, truly organic reforms" [243]. It seems to them that all social reform which might improve the workers' lot only consolidates the present system and postpones the revolution. Such an attitude may well become an obstacle to any immediate social progress.

Finally, the revolution considered as an objective, is too often used as an excuse to avoid doing something constructive to transform society. How many of those who are revolutionaries in spirit do not know what they would substitute for the system they want to overthrow or, if they do know, it is a dream of a system in which the working class would remain bound and enslaved to a state capitalism

(243) Pope Pius XII, Message of 1st September, 1944.

which would subjugate the whole world and transform labour into an enormous machine [244].

The social doctrine of the Church declares itself for "a progressive and prudent evolution, courageous and in conformity with nature, enlightened and guided by the holy Christian laws of justice and equity" [245].

But we must not think that it is only a question of a little touching up here and there and a few reforms which do not go to the root of the problem. On the contrary, the Church's social teaching aims at a complete transformation of society in its entire structure, of the social system and the social economy. It tends towards a radical renewal not only in institutions but — and this is how it differs from many reforms which are merely economic in objective — in the minds and hearts of men. Pius XI called for a complete *renewal* of the Christian spirit from which so many people engaged in industry have at times lamentably departed" [246] In the midst of war Pius XII analysed "the desire for *a new order*" and discerned a clear vision of the deficiencies of the present order and a deep desire for an order which would guarantee the juridical rules of national and international life [247]. He sought a new era for the *profound renewal and the complete reorganisation of the world*" [248]. A few years later he called for "*a profound and solid reconstruction of society*" [249], "*a new world*, a world ordered in its juridical structure, a more equitable and healthy world in which men would devote themselves to suppressing injustice and pursue motives of fraternal reconciliation rather than sources of discord or rancour" [250].

To this work, which Pius XII described as the *re-education of mankind* which should be spiritual and religious above all, starting

---

(244) Pope Pius XII, Allocution to Italian workers, 13th June, 1943.
(245) Quadragesimo Anno.
(246) Quadragesimo Anno.
(247) Radio Message, 24th December, 1940.
(248) Message, 25th December, 1944.
(249) Letter of 14th July, 1945, to M. Charles Flory.
(250) Pope Pius XII, Letter to the French Hierarchy, 8th January, 1945.

with Christ as its prerequisite foundation, realised by justice and crowned by charity [251], the Church brings the loyal and powerful support of her social teaching to enlighten men's minds and permeate their will, conscience and heart, "to bring man to obey the dictates of duty, to master their passions, to love God and his neighbour with a particular and sovereign charity and to overcome courageously all the obstacles which he meets in the path of virtue [252]. The instruments at the Church's disposal to reach souls — the sacraments, grace, the sacrifice of the Mass and the guidance of the Hierarchy — have been given to her by Jesus Christ Himself.

(251) Pope Pius XII, Encyclical, Summi Pontificatus, 20th October, 1939.
(252) Pope Leo XIII, Rerum Novarum.

CONCLUSION

The fundamental principles of the Church's social teaching are nothing but the expression of the natural law and reason, enlightened by Revelation [253].

1) To render to the *human person* his dignity, his true freedom and his rights. The social forms which make possible and guarantee full personal responsibility in the temporal as well as in the eternal order must be encouraged by all lawful means and in all spheres of life.

2) To defend, protect and restore *the family* in its economic, spiritual, moral and legal unity. To procure for it living-space, leisure and a home not too far from the place of work so that it can fulfil its mission to transmit new life, raise children and provide a family life which is both materially and spiritually good.

3) To give *work* the place in society marked out for it by God, to respect its dignity "as the indispensible means of conquering the world, the means designed by God for His glory" (Pius XII), the means of personal fulfilment and union between men. The pain and burden which it carries as a result of original sin does not destroy the dignity of work. But this dignity itself and the restoration of all things in Christ demand vigorous social action in the interests of the masses.

4) *To ensure that the workers and their families* have :

a) *living and working conditions* (wages, housing, private ownership) which redress injustice and render possible a better and more human life and security in the respect due to the dignity of the worker; — b) the opportunity for a human *culture;* — c) the place which the workers should hold *in the nation* side by side with the

(253) **Message of Pope Pius XII, 24th December, 1942.**

other classes so that they may "take their responsibility in the administration of the whole economy of the country" [254]. The aspirations of the workers coincide to a remarkable extent with the changes envisaged in the Church's social teaching.

5) To tend to *unify society* with loyal co-operation between different classes and professions by setting up a *vocational organisation* calculated to further the common good of the vocational group by more human, more just and more fraternal relations.

6) To develop a sense of the *common good* as a principle of unity by fighting against "the unbridled egoism which is the shame and great sin of our age" [255]. Then to encourage the extension of *social justice and charity* to institutions and laws so that they may serve the human person, its dignity and its destiny. To bring about a more equitable *distribution* of wealth and the national income in order to raise the standard of living of the less favoured classes.

7) To promote a true conception of *the State*. "No social institution, other than the family, is so vital and essential as the State. Its roots are in the order of creation and it is itself one of the constituent elements of the natural law" [256]. The State has the function of encouraging, helping and promoting the co-operation of all for the good of the whole community, neither absorbing the individual nor the family but, on the contrary, protecting their rights and freedoms, particularly if they are threatened. The State has the noble mission of being the guardian of rights of which it is not the origin. As it is the first servant and administrator of the common good it must be the first to respect it. Of course the complexity, extent and ramifications of national and international life today have considerably enlarged its sphere of action. This is but an added reason why the State should not abuse its powers or become totalitarian but should retain a true idea of its rôle and function.

(254) Pope Pius XII, Allocution to the Catholic Associations of Italian workers, 29th June, 1948.

(255) Pope Pius XI, Quadragesimo Anno.

(256) Pope Pius XII, Allocution to the Congress of Administration, 5th August, 1950.

8) *To correlate the juridical and moral orders*. Every man has the right to juridical security and this must not be threatened by arbitrary acts of the legislature, of the police or of the judiciary yielding to pressures of power or party. What is legal is not necessarily right — a law is not just merely because it has been voted by a parliament. The Creator has given a criterion to men's hearts to judge whether a law is just or not and this is the natural law, the light of reason based on the true nature of man and things and expressly confirmed by Revelation.

9) *To make the masses, an amorphous multitude of individuals, into a true people.*

The masses are not a people [257]. The masses are subject to external forces and are led without knowing where they go. A people lives from the fulness of the life of the men who compose it. In a people every citizen, in his own place, is a free person, cognizant of his dignity, responsibilities, convictions, rights and duties and mindful of the freedom and responsibilities of others.

In a true democracy the citizens have rights which authority should respect — the right to a personal opinion on the rights and duties which are imposed upon them, the right to be consulted and to have their opinion put into effect in a manner consistent with the common good. "The State should be the organic and organising unity of a true people" (Pius XII).

10) There can be no real social progress or civilisation without *reference to God and a return to the Gospel of Jesus Christ* as taught by the Church. The Church's social teaching recalls that, above and beyond the efforts of men or peoples or their governments to build the earthly city, there is the law of God and the Gospel to teach them the absolute order of beings and their purposes, the true hierarchy of values, an ideal of truth, justice and liberty and the need for all to share more justly in the world's goods, whether material, cultural or social. The Church's social teaching denounces the scandal of those Christians who outwardly practise their religion

(257) Pope Pius XII, Message of 24th December, 1944.

but do not yet understand that their salvation will depend on the way in which they practise justice and charity in their professional and social life. It imposes on Christians the duty of taking part in social and political developments which work for the transformation of the earthly city. It shows them the principles which should guide their action, the errors to be avoided, the spirit which should inspire them and the nobility and urgency of this social mission.

THE EXTENT OF THE SOCIAL TEACHING

Objection. Faced with this noble ideal there are already some who object : "all this is certainly very fine. But this ideal is so abstract, far-away and so completely in opposition to the whole structure of economic society and the complexity of the modern world that it is impossible to see how it could enlighten and guide Christians who are in the thick of the fight against the injustices of social life today".

The Church is the first to recognise that this ideal is in strong contrast to the world around us as we see it. That is why she makes bold to declare that there must be *"a complete reorganisation and a profound renewal of the world."* (Pius XII). Further, if we want to understand the grave reasons for the Popes' insistence on the pressing necessity and binding character of the Church's social teaching the ideal must be seen in all its dimensions and in the full extent of its objective. "The whole world must be re-made from its very foundations. From being inhuman it must be made human, from being human it must be made divine, that is to say, according to the Heart of God" [258]. In addition we have seen how the Popes have proclaimed that the structures of economic life are too often inhuman and that they crush the human person. *"The whole of economic life has become horribly harsh, implacable and cruel".* Who said that? — Pope Pius XI [259]. And again : *"Social life seems*

(258) Pope Pius XII, Radio Message, 10th February, 1952.
(259) Pope Pius XI, Encyclical, Quadragesimo Anno.

*to have become and enigma and an inextricable tangle"; "Society
is like a gigantic machine of which man is no longer the master
and which he even fears".* These were the words of Pius XII [260].

Finally, no-one knows better than the Church that the task of
"rebuilding a new world according to justice and love" [261] is hard
and difficult because, apart from the opposition of established
interests, she foresees the resistance that will come from human
weaknesses like sin, selfishness, hard hearts and cowardice. The
Church knows that much courage, initiative, enterprise and clear
thinking will be necessary for this battle. Pius XII called for *clear
vision, devotion, courage, inventive genius and fraternal charity
in all right and honest hearts,* to determine in what way and to what
extent the Christian spirit will succeed in maintaining and consoli-
dating the enormous work of the *restoration of social, economic
and international life* on a plane reconcilable with the religious
and moral content of Christian civilisation [262].

And again, addressing the Roman aristocracy; "Your rôle presupposes *much study, much work, much abnegation and above all,
much love"* [263]. In the same discourse the Pope denounced the
enemies of the task of construction; the desertion of those who held
themselves aloof, the abstention of the sullen or disgruntled man
who, discontented or discouraged, makes no use of his qualities
and energies, does not take part in any of the activities of his
country or of his time, but withdraws into his shell. . . the abstention
of indolent and passive indifference. . . the unconcern in the face
of ruin which threatens one's own brothers and people. This
abstention is never neutral, as those who indulge in it claim; "it is"
says the Pope, "whether we wish it or not, *an accessory".*

These are the moral qualities required from men of action of all
walks of life for this work of reconstruction.

The co-operation of men of learning and of scientific and

(260) Pope Pius XII, 20th February, 1946.
(261) Pope Pius XII, 20th October, 1939.
(262) Pope Pius XII, Message of 1st September, 1944.
(263) Pope Pius XII, Discourse of 8th February, 1947.

economists, sociologists, and specialists to apply her teaching to our epoch. They should keep the Hierarchy informed of the technical manner in which economic and social problems arise today, of the present state of economics and sociology and of the analysis of economic structures which weigh so heavily on moral, family and human life and which change remarkably quickly, particularly under the effects of the U.N.O. and its agencies and of the assistance given by better-off nations to under-developed areas.

A Final Objection

There remains one last, important objection to be answered. Some will say : "Of course we know the great Papal Encyclicals on the social teaching of the Church. But how many of the texts you have quoted are extracts from radio-messages or allocutions of Pope Pius XII. Now, even if we can accept that the Encyclicals have real authority, it does not necessarily follow — no matter how interesting these interventions may be — that we accept allocutions to pilgrims or to groups with a common interest like cyclists or tobacco planters etc. as having the same authority."

Reply—The Authority of Papal Documents.

There are several misapprehensions in this oft-repeated objection. In briefly explaining the following doctrinal points it will be easier to see the position of the social teaching of the Church and the authority with which the different papal documents are to be regarded by the faithful [264].

The living Magisterium of the Church exercises its teaching mission in two ways : 1) by extraordinary means; 2) by ordinary means

1) *By extraordinary means:* in a solemn and infallible judgement on a subject relating to faith and morals, by an Ecumenical Council economic experts is also necessary. The Church needs the help of

(264) The "Revue thomiste" (July-September 1956). An article on "Le magistère ordinaire du Souverain Pontife".

(the Sovereign Pontiff with the entire Episcopal College in communion with him) — or by the Pope speaking *ex cathedra,* i.e. as Pastor and Teacher of all Christians, by virtue of his supreme apostolic authority, and defining that a doctrine of faith or morals should be held by the Universal Church.

Such a judgement is infallible. Such a doctrine becomes dogma and he who rejects it is a heretic.

Because of the solemn character of this exceptional manner of teaching many Christians are tempted to consider it as the only rule of faith. This is a grave error which would considerably reduce the domain of the Church's authority; for such extraordinary intervention is quite exceptional (two or three times in a century) and is made only under particular conditions. Furthermore, a Papal pronouncement ought to be obeyed not only because it is infallible but because it is, to an extent which can be determined, the pronouncement of the Head of the Church, the Teacher and Pastor of the Universal Church, to which Jesus Christ has promised (in addition to the extraordinary and infallible help of the Holy Spirit in certain grave but rare circumstances) a continuing help for all time. "And behold I am with you all through the days that are coming, until the consummation of the world" (Mat. XXVIII. 20).

2) *By ordinary means. The encyclicals, allocutions and letters which Pius XII described as the documents in which the social teaching of the Church was to be mainly found are the normal channels of the ordinary Magisterium.* This is concerned not only with an isolated proposition of faith but with the whole of the living deposit of truths to be taught. This ordinary and universal magisterium is made up of the unanimous teaching of the Episcopal Body in communion with the Pope, each Bishop in his diocese and the Pope for the Universal Church, all teaching the truth. It is the normal process of Tradition.

Now there is here a true rule of faith which requires the adherence of the faithful who can advance from simple respect to a true act of faith. The teaching of the ordinary Magisterium can also be infallible; the Pope could choose to give a solemn definition by means of an Encyclical or even a radio message. Apart from these cases where infallibility may be exercised, the ordinary Magisterium is the *authentic* teaching which is binding on the faithful.

The Attitude of the faithful to the Teaching of the Ordinary Magisterium.

1) The most important thing is that faithful and clergy should have a particularly respectful, prudent, proper and receptive attitude towards any pronouncement of the Pope. The Head of the Church has the right to expect a responsive attitude. The truly faithful will immediately go further and put themselves in a general disposition of faith towards the mystery of the Church, believing that Jesus Christ invisibly guides His Church by the Holy Spirit and visibly by the Supreme Pontiff of the Universal Church, the Head and Teacher, the Pastor of all the Faithful. The Encyclical, *Humani Generis* laid down that the words of the Gospel, He who listens to you listens to me, also apply to whatever is taught by the ordinary Magisterium.

2) Those priests or layfolk, who then want to make an analysis of the document will seek to ascertain the degree of authority given by the Pope to his intervention and the obedience it calls for.

What is important in this aim is to *discover to what extent the Pope wishes to employ his authority in the document.* Did he merely want to sound a warning or to give advice? Did he want to indicate a positive direction or give a certain interpretation? Did he want to expound a doctrine in a positive manner or to settle a controversy, or to declare that such a matter was no longer to be considered an open question between theologians or, finally, to give a formal command?

The faithful may be surprised at first by these shades of meaning. On reflection they will understand the subtlety and discretion with which the authority of the living Magisterium is used and the respect it shows for the freedom of the children of God whom it has the mission to guide in a spirit of love.

But how are these degrees of authority to be recognised in the document itself?

Very often the expressions used by the Pope are themselves sufficient to make known his intention and will. Father Villain, in the book already mentioned, uses as an example the Letter of the Congregation of Council (1929) to Cardinal Lienart, which contains these different nuances : "The Church holds it morally necessary ... The Church exhorts... the Church wishes... the Church suggests... the Church recommends".

Then a *clear distinction must be made between the different parts of the document; the doctrinal part and the technical or economic part.* The Pope does not invoke his authority in those exposès, generally very brief, of a technical or economic touches doc-are delivered just to frame the question. But whatever touches doctrine on the contrary, belongs to the ordinary Magisterium.

Finally, the nature of the intervention of the Pope and the form chosen by him must be considered, whether it be an Encyclical, an allocution or a letter.

Of course the most solemn form is the Encyclical. For the Church's social teaching we know the great Encyclicals of Leo XIII (Rerum Novarum), Pius X (The Social Question), Pius XI (Quadragesimo Anno — Divini Redemptoris). Pius XII did not write a specific Encyclical on the social question but several of his Encyclicals, beginning with Summi Pontificatus, contain important passages on social problems.

Furthermore, Pius XII often preferred the form of radio message for his great teachings in order, as he explained it himself, to overcome by the spoken word the barriers raised by war, hot or cold, as regards written documents.

Now, contrary to what many think, *a radio message may have as much authority as an Encyclical.* Just think of the doctrinal riches of the great Christmas radio messages. With regard to them the duty of Christians is the same.

As for allocutions, it can be said that they are of two kinds.

In some the Pope particularly wants to reaffirm the Church's presence in contemporary life, his benevolent and paternal attention to different walks of life, his care as Pastor for their problems, their difficulties and their place in national life — these are the *pastoral* allocutions. (e.g. to pilgrimages and to certain professions). As against this, in other allocutions the Pope wants to give a true teaching on a doctrinal problem, not only to those present, but to all the faithful. These are the *doctrinal* allocutions. e.g. the discourses to doctors where Pius XII dealt with artificial insemination, therapeutic abortion, painless child-birth, anaesthesia, psychoanalysis etc., in short, a whole "deontology" was taught. On the plane of social teaching there are the discourses to different professions (employers, technicians, craftsmen, workers, farmers, businessmen etc. . . . .) or to Congresses (Financial, International Exchanges, Humanistic Studies, Administrative Sciences, International Law, etc.) or Letters to Social Study Weeks. All the documents which we have quoted fall into this category of *doctrinal* discourses, allocutions and letters.

3) When any document, no matter what its form (encyclical, radio-message, allocution or letter) is doctrinal in character, whenever the desire of the Holy Father to invoke his authority in pronouncing on some point of doctrine is obvious and wherever we find a true continuity in the teaching of successive Popes as in the case of the Church's social teaching, such an act of the ordinary Magisterium calls for acceptance and practical obedience on the part of the faithful. A respectful silence is not enough. Here again perhaps the living Magisterium can itself distinguish the degrees and shades in the expression of its intervention. But the faithful Christian who tries to conform dutifully to the intention and will of the head of the Church will receive this teaching in filial spirit, assimilate and practise it, taking the Pope's warnings and counsels into account. He will derive enlightenment, strength and courage to remain *himself* in the midst of the forces ranged against faith in the struggle of life. He will understand and often even discover for the first time his noble mission in the construction of a more human society. In the present confusion of minds and the dangers which threaten the world he will be proud to manifest the light of the social teaching of the Church and to benefit from her maternal care, anxious as she is to guide her children in the social, economic and political order which also affects the salvation of all mankind.

INDEX

Accommodation: 59
Agriculture: 81,107 124
Alcoholism: 138
Atomic Energy: 102
Authority of Papal documents: 160
Automation: 102

Baptism: 61
Berlin: 149
Birth-rate: 126
Blessed Trinity, The: 57
Bonuses: 131
Brotherhood of men: 62
Brotherhood of Nations: 74
Budapest: 149
Buying capacity: 98

Capital: 77, 79, 99, 145
Capitalism: 81, 146, 147, 149
Cartels: 123, 144
Catholic Action: 77, 139
Centralisation: 114
Centralisation of Industry: 102
    (see also "Industry" and "De-
    centralisation")
Charity: 23, 66, 67, 74, 77, 78,
    81, 93, 133, 134, 139, 140, 143,
    147, 153, 158, 159
Charity, Social: (see "Social Cha-
    rity")
Christian Civilisation: 40, 41, 159
Citizens, Duties and Rights of:
    135, 136, 138, 157
Civic Duties: 47
Classes: 118, 139, 156 (see "Work-
    ing Classes")
Class-warfare: 116, 120, 137, 147
Collective Administration: 149
Collective Enterprise: 102
Collective National Conventions:
    132
Collectivism: 82
Collectivist Economy: 127
Commerce: 107
Common Good, The: 37, 44, 66,
    67, 71, 75, 76, 78, 81, 85, 99,
    104, 113, 118, 121, 122, 127, 134,
    135, 137-139, 143, 145-147, 156,
    157
Communism: 27, 38, 58, 69, 83,
    145, 146-150
Communist Party: 147, 149, 150
    (see also "Twentieth Congress")
Communists: 148
Communist Socialism: 69 (see also

"Socialism")
Conscience: 140, 141, 143
Conservatism: 140
Consumer Goods: 76
Consumption: 98, 99
Co-partnership: 130-131

Decentralisation of Industry: 102
    (see also "Centralisation" and
    "Industry")
Democracy (a true): 157
Deposit of faith, The: 26
Destiny of man: 59, 139
Dictatorship: 55, 90, 149 (see also
    "Economic dictatorship")
Dignity of the human person: 54,
    55, 57, 60, 61, 73, 81, 155
Distinction of class: 62
Distribution of wealth: 30, 65, 67,
    68, 74, 75, 136, 156
Distributive justice: 112, 130, 135
    (see also "Justice")
Diversity of functions: 64, 66

Earthly City, The: 27, 30, 45, 158
Earthly Kingdom: 87
Economic Dictatorship: 137, 144
    (see also "Dictatorship")
Economists (18th and 19th cent.):
    95
Ecumenical Council: 160
Education: 32, 108
Emigration: 126
Employees: 132
Employers: 59, 63, 70, 85, 86, 116,
    118, 120, 121, 129, 132, (Note
    221) 138, 145
Employment, Conditions of: 83-84,
    155
Employment, Contract of: 60, 138
Employment, Dignity of: 155
Episcopal Body in communion
    with the Pope: 161

Equality of men: 53, 61-63, 68
Ethics: 31
Eucharist, The: 61
Faith: 47, 62, 129, 161, 164
Faith and Morals: 19, 160, 161
Family, The: 34, 35, 48, 55, 58,
    59, 65, 71, 73, 75, 77, 79, 81,
    87, 97, 102, 108, 110, 119, 143,
    155, 156, 160
Family Allowances: 138
Family holding, The: 81

Famine: 89
Fascism: 49
Farmer, The: 81
Fathers of the Church: 24
France: 21, 44, 103, 113
Fraternal Charity: 159 (see also "Charity")
Free competition for the maximum profit: 137, 143
Freedom of conscience: 44
French Hierarchy: 19, 20, 43, 49
Fundamental Human Rights: 26 (see also "Rights")
Fundamental Right 67, 71, 75 (see also "Rights")

Geography: 91
Germany: 44, 130
Gifts: 78
Gospels, The: 23, 157
Governments: 31
Grace: 140
Groups (Political): 106, (Professional): 106, (Specialised) 106

Health: 59, 96
Hierarchy: 153, 160 (see also "French Hierarchy")
Hierarchy of values: 142, 157
History: 48, 91
Hope: 47
Housing: 32, 98, 155
Human Culture: 155
Human Dignity: 51, 53, 57, 58, 145, 148 (see also "Dignity of the human person")
Human values: 126

I.L.O.: 46
Immigrants: 74
Imperialism: 42, 43
Incarnation, The: 36
Individualism: 143
Industrial Revolution: 30
Industry: 107, 124, 134, 144, 145, 148 (see also "Centralisation" and "Decentralisation")
Inequality (of conditions): 64
Inequality (of individuals): 64
Injustice: 152, 155
Injustice, Social: 30, 140, 152
Insurance against accidents, unemployment, sickness, disability, old age, etc.: 138
International relations: 91

Investments: 78

Judicial Order: 45, 137
Judicial status: 106
Juridical Order: 34, 157
Jugoslavia: 127
Justice: 23, 66, 67, 74, 79, 81, 85, 112, 117, 122, 129, 134, 135, 138, 140, 143, 152, 153, 157, 158, 159 (see also "Social Justice")
Justice and Equity: 152
Just wage: 60

Khrushchev: 147

Labour: 131, 152
Labour Exchanges: 87
Laissez-faire: 140
Last Judgement, The: 77
Legal Order, The: 130
Legal Structure (of economic and social life): 122
Leo XIII: 33, 40, 43, 58-62, 67, 82, 85, 105, 107, 109, 111, 118, 124, 144, 163
Liberal Capitalism: 99, 142, 144-146 (see also "Capitalism")
Liberal Economy: 69
Liberalism: 27, 49, 81, 83, 113, 141, 143
Liberalism (Capitalistic): 142
Liberalism (Economic): 142-143
Living Conditions: 74
Living space: 155 (see also " Minimal living space")

Magisterium, The living: 21, 24, 25, 26, 49, 50, 160, 162, 164
Magisterium, The Ordinary: 161-164
Management: 121, 131
Man's fundamental needs: 97, 98
Man's vocation: 97, 100
Marx: 100, 146, 147
Marxism: 49
Marxist Communism: 142, 146 (see also "Communism")
Masses, The: 72, 77, 108, 155, 157
Materialism: 42
Material Prosperity: 142
Mechanisation: 81
Medicine: 91
Mergers: 144
Middle Ages: 41

Minimal living space: 73, 79 (see also "Living space")
Mission of the Church: 29, 30, 38, 39, 42, 50, 93
Monopolies: 123
Moral Law: 26, 29, 32, 76, 77, 85, 93, 102, 137, 141-150
Moral Order: 108, 157
Mystical Body, The: 23, 29, 38, 66, 115, 140

National Income: 121, 156
Nationalisation: 128-129
Natural Law, The: 21, 22, 46, 47, 78, 81, 130, 145, 156, 157
Natural Order: 35, 36, 37
Nazism: 26, 27, 38, 63, 71
New Testament: 23

Occupational risks: 59, 85
Old Testament: 22
Organic concept of Society: 136
Organic unity of a true people: 157
Organisational Experts: 126
Original Sin: see "Sin"
Ownership: 80
Ownership (Concept of): 129
Ownership (Private): 79-82, 146, 155
Ownership (Right of): 73, 74, 75, 78, 80, 81, 146

Pius X: 163
Pius XI: 32, 45, 55, 59, 63, 67, 68, 79, 80, 82, 85, 86, 88, 99, 101, 109, 111, 113, 118, 128, 134, 135, 139, 144, 145, 152, 158, 163
Pius XII: 19, 22, 24, 28, 31-35, 41, 42, 45-49, 51, 55-57, 60, 63, 64, 67-69, 70, 71, 74, 75, 78, 80, 81, 82, 84, 86, 87, 89, 90, 91, 95, 96, 98-100, 101, 104, 106, 110, 112, 114, 115, 116, 119, 122, 124, 128-130, 134, 135, 137, 138, 141, 145, 146, 147, 152, 155, 157-160, 163, 164,
Planning: 124-127
Political Movements: 59
Political Parties: 127 (see also "Groups-Political")
Poznam: 149
Prices: 138
Private Enterprise: 87, 124

Private and Public Rights: 123, 129, 130
Private Property: 72, 73, 75, 76, 79
Production: 98, 100, 116, 124, 131
Productive Resources: 128
Productivity: 96
Profit sharing: 131
Proletariat, The: 68, 72, 144
Prophets, The: 23
Prudence: 137
Public Bodies: 58
Public Order: 106-107
Purchasing Power: 100

Racial Segregation: 63
Raw materials, capital and man-power: 138
Reason: 129, 155, 157
Reconstruction of Society: 152, 159
Redemption, The: 51, 140
Reforms in practice: 151-153
Re-organisation and renewal of the world: 152, 158
Revelation: 21-23, 26, 33, 46, 47, 155, 157
Right of Association: 30, 71
Rights: see "Fundamental..."
Rights (Human): 34, 69, 70, 71, 79, 100, 117, 147
Rights (of Man): 53, 71
Rights (of the person): 31, 34, 55, 58, 59, 60, 64, 65, 69, 109, 110, 114, 146, 147, 155
Rights (of Women): 59, 65
Rights (of Workers): 86
Right to Work: 82-88
Rule of Faith: 161

Saint Paul: 115
Saint Thomas: 76 (note 105)
Scientific and economic experts: 159
Secularism: 42, 43
Servants: 61, 62
Sharing the Wealth: 107, 136, 157
Sin: 23, 67, 149, 150, 156, 159
Sin, Original: 36, 88, 90, 143, 155
Social Charity: 139, 140, 156
Socialism: 83, 149
Socialist International: 72
Socialists: 84
Social Justice: 67, 75, 78, 79, 93, 110, 117, 122, 133-138, 145, 156 (see "Justice")

Social Mission of Christians: 158
Social Order: 137, 164
Social Progress: 140, 151
Social Revolution: 151
Social Thought (different schools of): 24-25
Sociology: 32, 45, 91, 160
Soviet Russia: 44, 72, 127, 147, 148
Stalin: 127, 147-150
Standard of living: 100, 107, 156
State, The: 28, 35, 37, 42-44, 48, 69, 71, 74, 76, 79, 83, 84, 87, 90, 96, 99, 107, 111-113, 118, 120, 123-128, 130, 131, 135, 139, 156, 157
State (Ownership): 128
State Capitalism: 151 (see also "Capitalism")
State, The Christian: 33
Station in life (Man's): 29
Statism: 114
Strikes: 117
Supernatural Order: 35, 37
Surplus Wealth: 78 (note 105)

Technocracy: 27, 90, 125
Technocrats: 127
Technology: 96
Temperance: 137
Temporal Order: 108
Thomas, St.: 76 (note 105)
Totalitarianism: 27, 147
Totalitarian States: 55, 95, 99, 127, 156 (see also "The State")
Town Planning: 102
Trade Unionism: 59
Trade Unions: 59, 70, 120, 143
Trade War: 143
Tradition (the normal process of): 161
Transport: 32
Trusts: 123, 144
Twentieth Congress of the Communist Party of the Soviet Union: 147 (see also "Communist Party")

Under-developed areas: 160
Unemployed (The): 78
Unemployment: 87, 138
Unemployment (Fight against): 87
Unity: 34
Unity (of men of good-will): 35, 87

Unity (of purpose and action): 115
Unity (of the community): 116
Unity (through work): note 117
U.N.O.: 160
Usury: 78

Vatican Council: 22
Vocational Organisation: 27, 35, 85, 118, 119, 120-123, 131-133, 138, 143, 156

Wage-contract: 130
Wage-earners: 112, 129
Wage, Family: 86
Wage, Living: 85-86
Wages: 59, 60, 84, 85, 86, 121, 138, 155
War: 177, 129, 150, 152, 153,
Weekly day of rest: 144
Work (Conditions of): 83-84, 155
Work: (Dignity of): 155
Work (Exploitation of): 146
Work (Nobility of): 34
Workers, The: 32, 59, 63, 68, 70, 73, 82, 84, 85, 86, 88, 89, 99, 100, 116, 117, 118, 120, 121, 131, 137, 143, 144, 146, 147, 151, 155, 156
Working-class: 117, 131, 148, 149, 151
Working Conditions: 132, 155
Working Conditions (of women and children): 144
Working-hours: 144

BIBLIOGRAPHY

The Functional Economy *by Bernard William Dempsey published by Prentice Hall.*

Communism and Christianity *by Martin D'Arcy, published by Penguin. (1956).*

Policy for the West *by Barbara Ward, Penguin.*

Christian Humanism *by Louis Bouyer, published by Geoffrey Chapman.*

The Springs of Morality *A Catholic Symposium, Edited by John. M. Todd, published by Burns & Oates.*

Marxism Past and Present *by R. N. Carew Hunt, published by Geoffrey Bles.*

The Theory and Practice of Communism *by R. N. Carew Hunt, published by Geoffrey Bles.*

God, Man and the Universe — A Christian Answer to Modern Materialism *A selection of essays edited by Jacques de Bivort la Saudee, published by Burns & Oates.*

A Map of Life *by F. J. Sheed, published by Sheed & Ward.*

Economic Control *by Michael Fogarty, published by Routledge & Keegan Paul.*

Church and State *by L. Sturzo, published by Geoffrey Bles.*

Code of Social Principles *3rd Ed. English translation published by Catholic Social Guild, 1952.*

Communism and Man, *F. J. Sheed, published by Sheed & Ward.*

Welfare and Taxation, *Colin Clark, published by Catholic Social Guild, 1954.*

The Whole Man Goes to Work, *by Henry L. Nunn, published by Harpers & Brothers (New York).*

Philosophy of Value *by Leo R. Ward, Burns Oates & Washbourne.*

The translation of Quadragesimo Anno and Rerum Novarum used throughout was taken from the "The Social Order" and "The Workers' Charter" published jointly by the Catholic Truth Society and The Catholic Social Guild, Oxford. The translation of the great Christmas Message of Pope Pius XII of 1942 is that of Canon George Smith published also by the Catholic Truth Society.

"MATER ET MAGISTRA"

ENCYCLICAL LETTER OF POPE JOHN XXIII

ENCYCLICAL LETTER OF POPE JOHN XXIII
ON RECENT DEVELOPMENTS
OF THE SOCIAL QUESTION
IN THE LIGHT OF CHRISTIAN TEACHINGS

Mother and Teacher of all nations, the universal Church has been instituted by Jesus Christ so that all who in the long course of centuries come to her loving embrace may find fullness of higher life and a guarantee of salvation. To this Church, "the pillar and ground of truth," her most holy Founder has entrusted the double task of begetting children and of educating and governing them, guiding with maternal providence the life both of individuals and of peoples, the dignity of which she has always held in the highest respect and guarded with watchful care. Christianity is truly a joining together of earth with heaven in that it takes man concretely, spirit and matter, intellect and will, and invites him to raise his mind above the changing conditions of earthly existence to the heights of eternal life which will be consummated in unending happiness and peace. Hence although the Holy Church has the special task of sanctifying souls and making them participants in the good of the supernatural order, she is also solicitous for the exigencies of the daily life of men, not merely those concerning the nourishment of the body and the material conditions of life but also those that concern prosperity and culture in all its many aspects and stages.

In this activity the Church is carrying out the command of her Founder, Christ, who refers primarily to man's eternal salvation when He says, "I am the way, and the truth, and the life" and "I am the light of the world." On other occasions, however, seeing the hungry crowd He was moved to exclaim, "I have compassion on this multitude," thereby showing that He was also concerned about the earthly needs of men. The Divine Redeemer shows this care not only by His words but also by the actions of His life, as when to alleviate the hunger of the crowds He several times miraculously multiplied bread. By means of this bread given for the nourishment of the body, He wished to preannounce that heavenly food of the soul which He was to give to men on the vigil of His Passion. It is no wonder, then, that the Church in imi-

tation of Christ and in fulfilment of His command, has for two
thousand years, from the institution of the early Deacons to the
present time, held aloft the torch of charity by her teaching and
her generous example, that charity which, by harmoniously blend-
ing together the precepts and the practice of mutual love, puts into
effect in a wonderful way the commandment of the twofold giving
by word and by deed in which is summarised the social teaching
and activity of the Church. An outstanding instance of this teaching and action carried on by the Church throughout the ages is
undoubtedly the immortal Encyclical *Rerum Novarum,* issued
seventy years ago by Our Predecessor Leo XII of happy memory
to enunciate the principles acording to which the status of the
worker could be settled in a Christian manner.

Seldom have the words of a Pontiff had such universal repercussions on account of the profundity of the arguments used, their
scope and incisiveness. Indeed these directives and appeals have
had such importance that they can never fall into oblivion. A new
path was opened for the action of the Church, whose Supreme
Pastor by making his own the sufferings, cries and aspirations of
the lowly and oppressed, once again constituted himself the guardian of their rights. Even today, in spite of the long lapse of time,
the power of that Message is still operative in the documents of
the Popes who succeeded Leo XIII and who in their social teaching repeatedly return to the Leonine Encyclical, at one time to
draw inspiration from it, at another to clarify its application, but
always to find in it a stimulus to Catholic activity. That power
is also operative in the actual legislation of nations. This is a sign
that the solidly grounded principles, the historical directives and
the paternal appeals contained in the masterly Encyclical of Our
Predecessor preserve today their value, and even suggest new and
vital criteria so that men can judge the nature and extent of the
social question as it presents itself today and can face and meet
their respective responsibilities.

The period of the Encyclical "Rerum Novarum"
Leo XIII spoke in a time of radical transformation, of height-
ened contrasts and of bitter revolt. The shadows cast by that period
enable us to appreciate more accurately the light that radiated
from his teaching. As is well known, the conception of the economic
world that was most widely accepted at that time and very largely

carried out in practice, was a naturalistic one that denied any relation between economic activity and morality. It was alleged that
the only motive of economic action was personal profit. The supreme rule regulating the relations between economic agents was
free competition without limit. Interest on capital, prices of goods
and services, profits and wages, were determined purely mechanic-
ally by the laws of the market. The State, it was held, should re-
frain from all intervention in the economic field. Trade unions,
according to the conditions of the different countries, were either
forbidden, tolerated or considered to have legal personality in private law. In an economic world thus constituted, the law of the
strongest was fully justified on theoretical grounds, and in practice
governed the concrete relations between men. There thus, resulted
an economic order that was radically deranged. While enormous
riches accumulated in the hands of a few, the working classes
found themselves in conditions of increasing hardship. Wages were
insufficient or at starvation level, conditions of work were oppressive and without respect for physical health, moral behaviour and
religious faith. Especially inhuman were the working conditions
to which children and women were subjected. The spectre of unemployment was ever present and the family was exposed to a
process of disintegration. Hence, there was widespread dissatis-
faction among the working classes, among whom a spirit of protest
and revolt permeated and grew stronger. All these things explain
why among these classes extremist theories that propounded remedies worse than the evil to be cured, found widespread favour.

In such difficult times, it was for Leo XII to proclaim his social message based on the real nature of man and animated by the
principles and spirit of the Gospel, a message that on its very appearance, in spite of some understandable opposition, aroused widespread admiration and enthusiasm. This was certainly not the first
time that the Apostolic See descended into the arena of earthly
interests in defence of the needy. Other documents of Leo XIII
had previously marked out the path, but here was formulated an
organic synthesis of principles joined to such a wide historical perspective that the Encyclical *Rerum Novarum* became a summary
of Catholicism in the economico-social field. This action was not
without hazard, because while some alleged that the Church, face
to face with the social question, should confine herself to preaching
resignation to the poor and to exhorting the rich to generosity,

Leo XIII did not hesitate to proclaim and defend the legitimate rights of the worker. At the outset of his exposition of Catholic teaching on social matters, he solemnly declared, "We approach the subject with confidence and in the exercise of the rights which belong to Us. For no practical solution of this question will ever be found without the assistance of Religion and the Church."

To You, Venerable Brethren, are well known those basic principles, expounded with as much authority as clarity by the immortal Pontiff, according to which the economico-social sector of human society should be reconstituted.

They first and foremost concern work, which ought to be valued and treated not just as a commodity but as an expression of the human person. For the great majority of mankind, work is the only source from which they draw means of livelihood and so its remuneration cannot be left to the mechanical play of market forces. Instead, it should be determined by justice and equity, which otherwise would be profoundly harmed even if the contract of work should have been freely entered into by both parties. Private property, including that of productive goods, is a natural right which the State cannot suppress. Embedded within it, is a social function, and it is, thus, a right that is exercised for one's personal benefit and for the good of others.

The State, the reason for whose existence is the realisation of the common good in the temporal order, cannot keep aloof from the economic world. It should be present to promote in a suitable manner the production of a sufficient supply of material goods, "the use of which is necessary for the practice of virtue," and to watch over the rights of all citizens, especially of the weaker, such as workers, women and children. It is also its ineluctable task to contribute actively to the betterment of the condition of life of the workers. It is further the duty of the State to secure that work relations be regulated according to justice and equity and that in the environment of work the dignity of the human being be not violated in body or spirit. On this point attention is drawn to the guiding lines of the Leonine Encyclical on which the social legislation of modern Nations has been patterned, and which, as Pius XI already noted in the Encyclical *Quadragesimo Anno,* have contributed efficaciously to the rise and development of a new and most desirable branch of jurisprudence, namely Labour Law. In the Encyclical the right of the workers alone, or of groups made up of workers and owners, to associate, is declared to be natural, as are also the right to adopt that organisational structure which the workers consider most suitable to attain their legitimate economic-professional interests, and the right to act autonomously and by personal initiative within the association for the achievement of these ends.

Workers and employers should regulate their mutual relations under the inspiration of the principle of human solidarity and Christian brotherhood, because both competition in the liberal sense and the class struggle in the Marxist sense, are contrary to nature and the Christian conception ol life. These, Venerable Brethren, are the fundamental principles on which a healthy economico-social order can be built. It is not surprising, therefore, that the more ably endowed Catholics, responsive to the appeals of the Encyclical, began many activities in order to translate these principles into reality. Indeed, under the impulse of objective needs of a similar nature, men of good will from all nations of the earth were also moved to act in a similar manner. For these reasons, the Encyclical was rightly acknowledged as the Magna Charta of the economico-social reconstruction of the modern era.

The Encyclical "Quadragesimo Anno"

Pius XI, Our Predecessor of holy memory, after a lapse of forty years commemorated the Encyclical *Rerum Novarum* with another solemn document, the Encyclical *Quadragesimo Anno*. In it the Supreme Pontiff confirmed the right and duty of the Church to make its irreplaceable contribution to the correct solution of the pressing and grave problems that beset the human family. He confirms the fundamental principles and the historic directives of the Leonine Encyclical. In addition, he took the opportunity to make more precise some points of that teaching on which even among Catholics some doubts had arisen, and to reformulate Christian social thought in response to the changed conditions of the times. The doubts that had thus arisen concerned particularly private property, the wage system, and the attitude of Catholics towards a type of moderate socialism. Concerning private property, Our Predecessor reaffirms its place in natural law and emphasises its social aspect with its corresponding function. Turning to the wage system, he rejects the view that would declare it unjust by its very nature; but at the same time, he condemns the inhuman and unjust forms under which it is often found. He repeats and enlarges upon the criteria to be used and the conditions to be satisfied if the wage system is not to violate justice or equity. On this point, Our Predecessor clearly points out that, in the present circumstances, it is advisable that the contract of work be modified by elements taken from the contract of partnership, in such a way that "the wage earners are made sharers in some sort in the ownership, or the management, or the profits." Of the greatest doctrinal and practical importance is his affirmation that "if the social and individual character of labour be overlooked, it can be neither equitably appraised nor properly recompensed according to strict justice." Hence, the Pope declares that, in determining wages, justice requires that, in addition to the needs of the individual workers and their family responsibilities, one should also consider both the conditions in the productive organisations in which the workers carry on their labour and the demands of "the public economic good."

He emphasises that the opposition between Communism and Christianity is fundamental, and makes it clear that Catholics are in no way permitted to be supporters of moderate socialism because its concept of life is bounded by time, inasmuch as it places its supreme objective in the welfare of society, and either because it proposes a form of social structure that aims solely at production, thus causing grave loss to human liberty, or because it lacks every principle of true social authority. Pius XI was not unaware that, in forty years that had passed since the appearance of the Leonine Encyclical, historical conditions had profoundly altered. In fact, free competition, due to its own intrinsic tendencies, had ended in almost destroying itself. It had caused a great accumulation of wealth and a corresponding concentration of economic power in the hands of a few who "are frequently not the owners, but only the trustees and directors of invested funds, who administer them at their good pleasure." Therefore, as the Pope discerningly notes, "free competition is dead; economic dictatorship has taken its place. Unbridled ambition for domination has succeeded the desire for gain; the whole economic life has become hard, cruel and relentless in a ghastly measure," thus subjecting the public authority to the interests of groups and issuing forth in international imperialism in financial affairs.

To remedy such a state of affairs, the Pope points out as fundamental the reinstatement of the economic world in the moral order and the striving for individual or group interests within the framework of the common good. This implied, according to his teaching, the reconstruction of human society by the reconstituting of intermediate bodies autonomous in their economico-professional range, not imposed by the State but created by the respective members. Public authority should resume its duty of promoting the common good of all. Finally, there should be co-operation on a world scale even in economic matters among the nations.

The fundamental points that characterise the masterly Encyclical of Pius XI can be reduced to two. The first is that one cannot take as the supreme criterion of economic activities and institutions the interest of individuals or of groups, nor free competition nor economic power, nor the prestige or power of the nation, nor other similar criteria. Instead, the supreme criterion of such activities and institutions are justice and social charity. The second is that men should strive to achieve a national and international juridical order, with a complexus of public and private permanent institutions, inspired by social justice, one to which the economic sector should conform, thus making it less difficult for economic agents to carry out their tasks in conformity to the demands of justice and within the framework of the common good.

Radio Message of Pentecost 1941

In defining and developing the Christian social doctrine great contributions have been made by Pope Pius XII, Our Predecessor of venerable memory, who on the feast of Pentecost, June 1st, 1941, broadcast a message "in order to call to the attention of the Catholic world a memory worthy of being written in letters of gold on the Calendar of the Church : the fiftieth anniversary of the publication of the epoch-making social Encyclical of Leo XIII the *Rerum Novarum*" . . . and "to render to Almighty God from the bottom of Our heart, Our humble thanks for the gift, which . . . He bestowed on the Church in that Encyclical of His Vicar on earth and to praise Him for the lifegiving breath of the Spirit which through it, in ever-growng measure from that time on, has blown on all mankind." In the Radio Message the great Pontiff claims for the Church "the indisputable competence" to "decide whether the bases of a given social system are in accord with the unchangeable order which God our Creator and has shown us through the Natural Law and Revelation." He confirms the perennial vi-

tality and inexhaustible richness of the teachings of the Encyclical
Rerum Novarum. He takes the occasion "to give some further directive moral principles on three fundamental values of social and
economic life. These three fundamental values which are closely
connected one with the other, mutually complementarly and dependent, are : the use of material goods, labour and the family."
Concerning the use of material goods, Our Predecessor declares that
the right of every man to use them for his own sustenance is prior
to every other right of economic import and so is prior to the right
of property. Undoubtedly, adds Our Predecessor, the right to property in material goods is also a natural right. Nevertheless, in
the objective order established by God, the right to property should
be so arranged that it is not an obstacle to the satisfaction of "the
unquestionable needs that the goods, which were created by God
for all men, should flow to all alike, according to the principles
of justice and charity."

Taking up a point that occurs in the Leonine Encyclical, Pius
XII declares that work is at one and the same time a duty and
a right of every human being. Consequently, it is for men in the
first place to regulate their mutual relations in work. Only in the
event that the interested parties do not or cannot fulfil their functions, does "it fall back on the State to intervene in the field of
labour and in the division and distribution of work according to
the form and measure that the common good properly understood
demands." In dealing with the family the Supreme Pontiff affirms
that private property of material goods is also considered as being
linked with "the existence and development" of the family, that
is to say, an apt means "to secure for the father of a family the
healthy liberty he needs in order to fulfil the duties assigned him
by the Creator regarding the physical, spiritual and religious welfare of the family." In this also is included the right to emigrate.
On this point Our Predecessor observes that when the States, both
those that permit emigration and those that accept immigrants, try
to eliminate "as far as possible all obstacles to the birth and growth
of real confidence" among themselves, mutual advantages result,
and together they contribute to the well-being of mankind and the
progress of culture.

Further changes
The situation, already changed during the period mentioned

by Pius XII, has undergone in these two decades profound trans-
formations both in the internal structure of each political community and in their mutual relations. In the field of science, technology, and economics : the discovery of nuclear energy, its application first to the purposes of war and later its increasing employment
for peaceful ends; the unlimited possibilities opened up by chemistry in synthetic products; the growth of automation in the sectors
of industry and services; the modernisation of the agricultural sector; the virtual disappearance of distances through communication
effected especially by radio and television; the increased speed in
transportation; the initial conquests of interplanetary space. In the
social field : the development of systems for social insurance and,
in some more economically advanced political communities, the
introduction of social security systems; in labour movements the
formation of, and the increased importance attached to, a more
responsible attitude towards the greater social-economic problems;
a progressive improvement of basic education; an ever wider distribution of welfare; an increased social mobility and the resulting
decline in the divisions among the classes; the interest in world
events on the part of those with an average education. Furthermore, the increased efficiency of economic systems in a growing
number of political communities helps to underscore the lack of
economico-social balance between the agricultural sector on the
one hand and the sector of industry and services on the other;
between economically developed and less developed areas within
the individual political communities; and on a world-wide plane,
the even more pronounced social-economic inequality existing between economically advanced countries and those in the process
of development. In the political field : the participation in public
life in many political communities of an increasing number of citizens coming from diverse social strata; a more extensive and
deeper activity of public authorities in the economic and social
field. To these must also be added, on the international level, the
end of colonial regimes and the attainment of political independence by the peoples of Asia and Africa; the growth of close relationships between the peoples and a deepening of their interdependence; the appearance on the scene and development of an
ever-growing network of organisations with a world-wide scope and
inspired by supranational criteria : organisations with economic,
social, cultural and political ends.

L

Reasons for the new Encyclical

Therefore, We feel it Our duty to keep alive the torch lighted by Our great Predecessors and to exhort all to draw from its inspiration and orientation in the search for solutions to the social problems more adapted to our times. For this reason, on the occasion of the solemn commemoration of the Leonine Encyclical, We are happy to have the opportunity to confirm and specify points of doctrine already treated by Our Predecessors, and, at the same time, to elucidate further the mind of the Church with respect to the new and more important problems of the day.

EXPLANATION AND DEVELOPMENT
OF THE TEACHING IN THE "RERUM NOVARUM"

First of all, it should be affirmed that the economic order is the creation of the personal initiative of private citizens themselves working either individually or in association with each other in various ways for the prosecution of common interest. But here, for the reasons Our Predecessors have pointed out, the public authorities must not remain inactive, if they are to promote in a proper way the productive development on behalf of social progress for the benefit of all the citizens. Their action whose nature is to direct, stimulate, co-ordinate, supply and integrate, should be inspired by the "principle of subsidiarity," formulated by Pius XI in the Encyclical *Quadragesimo Anno* : "This is a fundamental principle of social philosophy, unshaken and unchangeable . . . just as it is wrong to withdraw from the individual and commit to the community at large what private enterprise and industry can accomplish, so too it is an injustice, a grave evil, and a disturbance of right order for a larger and higher organisation to arrogate to itself functions which can be performed efficiently by smaller and lower bodies. . . . Of its very nature, the true aim of all social activity should be to help individual members of the social body, but never to destroy or absorb them." It cannot be denied that today the development of scientific knowledge and productive technology offers the public authorities concrete possibilities of reducing the inequality between the various sectors of production, between the various areas of political communities, and between the various countries themselves on a world-wide scale. This development also puts it within their capability to control fluctuations in the economy and, with hope of success, to prevent the recurrence of massive unemployment. Consequently, those in authority, who are responsible for the common good, feel the need not only to exercise in the field of economics a multiform action, at once more vast, more profound, more organic, but also it is necessary for this same end, that they give themselves suitable structures, tasks, means and methods.

But the principle must always be reaffirmed that the presence of the State in the economic field, no matter how widespread and penetrating, must not be exercised so as to reduce evermore the sphere of freedom for the personal initiative of individual citizens, but rather so as to guarantee in that sphere the greatest possible scope by the effective protection for each and all, of the essential personal rights; among which is to be numbered the right that individual persons possess of being always primarily responsible for their own upkeep and that of their own family; which implies that in the economic systems the free development of productive activities should be permitted and facilitated. For the rest, historic evolution itself puts into relief ever more clearly that there cannot be a well-ordered and fruitful society without the support in the economic field both of the individual citizen and of the public authorities; a working together in harmony in the proportions corresponding to the needs of the common good in the changing situations and vicissitudes of human life. Experience, in fact, shows that where the personal initiative of individuals is lacking, there is political tyranny; and there is also stagnation in the economic sectors engaged in the production especially of the wide range of consumer goods and of services which pertain, in addition to material needs, to the requirements of the spirit; goods and services which call into play in a special way the creative talents of individuals. While, where the due services of the State are lacking or defective, there is incurable disorder, and exploitation of the weak on the part of the unscrupulous strong who flourish in every land and at all times, like the cockle among the wheat.

SOCIAL ACTION

Origin and Scope of the Phenomenon
    One of the typical aspects which characterise our epoch is
social action, understood as the progressive multiplication of relations in society, with different forms of life and activity, and juridical institutionalisation. This is due to many historical factors,
among which must be numbered technical and scientific progress,
a greater productive efficiency and a higher standard of living
among the citizens. Social action is, at one and the same time, an
effect and a cause of growing intervention of the public authorities
in even the most crucial matters such as those concerning the care
of health, the instruction and education of the younger generation,
and the controlling of professional careers and the methods of
care and rehabilitation of those variously handicapped; but it is
also the fruit and expression of a natural tendency, almost irre-
pressible, in human beings, the tendency to join together to attain
objectives which are beyond the capacity and means at the disposal
of single individuals. A tendency of this sort has given life, especially in these last decades, to a wide range of groups, movements,
associations and institutions with economic, cultural, social, sport-
ing, recreational, professional and political ends, both within single
national communities and on an international level.

Evaluation
    It is clear that social action, so understood, brings many ad-
vantages. It makes possible, in fact, the satisfaction of many personal rights especially those called economico-social such as, for
example, the right to the indispensable means of human maintenance, to health services, to instruction at a higher level, to a more
thorough professional formation, to housing, to work, to suitable
leisure, to recreation. In addition, through the ever more perfect
organisation of the modern means for the diffusion of thought—
press, cinema, radio, television—it is made possible for individuals
to take part in human events on a world-wide scale. At the same
time, however, social action multiplies the forms of organisation
and makes the juridical control of relations between men of every
walk of life ever more detailed. As a consequence, it restricts the
range of the individual as regards his liberty of action; and uses
means, follows methods and creates an atmosphere which makes

it difficult for each one to think independently of outside influences, to work of his own initiative, to exercise his responsibility, to affirm and enrich his personality. Ought it to be concluded, then, that social action, growing in extent and depth, necessarily reduces men to automatons? It is a question which must be answered negatively. For social action is not to be considered as a product of natural forces working in a deterministic way; it is, on the contrary, as we have observed, a creation of men; beings conscious, free and intended by nature to work in a responsible way, even if in their so acting they are obliged to recognise and respect the laws of economic development and social progress and cannot escape from all the pressures of their environment. Hence, we consider that social action can and ought to be realised in such a way as to draw from it the advantages contained therein and to remove or restrain the negative aspects.

For this purpose, then, it is required that a sane view of the common good be present and operative in men invested with public authority: a view which is formed by all those social conditions which permit and favour for the human race the integral development of human personality. Moreover, we consider necessary that the intermediary bodies and the numerous social enterprises in which above all social action tends to find its expression and its activity, enjoy an effective autonomy in regard to the public authorities and pursue their own specific interests in loyal collaboration between themselves, subordinately, however, to the demands of the common good. For it is no less necessary that the above mentioned groups present the form and substance of a true community, that is, that the individual members be considered and treated as persons and encouraged to take an active part in ordering of their lives.

In the development of the organisation of modern society, order is realised ever more with a renewed balance between the need of autonomous and active collaboration of all, individuals and groups, and the timely co-ordination of the direction of the public authority.

So long as social action confines its activity within the limits of the moral order, along the lines indicated, it does not, of its nature, entail serious dangers of restriction to the detriment of individual human beings; rather, it helps to promote in them the expression and development of truly personal characteristics; it produces, too, an organic reconstruction of society, which Our Predecessor Pius XII in the Encyclical *Quadragesimo Anno* put forward and defended as the indispensable prerequisite for the satitfying of the demands of social justice.

REMUNERATION OF WORK

Standards of Justice and Equity

Our heart is filled with a deep sadness in contemplating the immeasurably sorrowful spectacle of vast numbers of workers in many lands and entire continents, who are paid wages which condemn them and their families to sub-human conditions of life. This is doubtless due, among other reasons, to the fact that in these countries and continents the process of industrialisation is just beginning or is still insufficiently developed.

In some of these countries, however, there stands in harsh and offensive contrast to the wants of the great majority the abundance and unbridled luxury of the privileged few; in still other countries the present generation is compelled to undergo inhuman privations in order to increase the output of the national economy at a rate of acceleration which goes beyond the limits permitted by justice and humanity, while in other countries a notable percentage of income is absorbed in building up or furthering an ill-conceived national prestige, or vast sums are spent on armaments. Moreover, in the economically developed countries, it not rarely happens that whilst great, or sometimes very great, remuneration is made for the performance of some small task or one of doubtful value, yet the diligent and profitable work of whole classes of decent hard-working men receives a payment that is much too small, insufficient or in no way corresponding to their contribution to the good of the community, or to the profit of the undertakings in which they are engaged, or to the general national economy. We judge it, therefore, to be Our duty to reaffirm once again that the remuneration of work, just as it cannot be left entirely to the laws of the market; so neither can it be fixed arbitrarily; it must rather be determined according to justice and equity. This requires that the workers should be paid a wage which allows them to live a truly human life and to fulfil with dignity their family responsibilities; but it requires, too, that in the assessment of their remuneration regard be had to their effective contribution to the pro-

duction and to the economic state of the enterprise; to the requirement of the common good of the respective political communities,
especially with regard to the repercussions on the overall employment of the labour force in the entire country; as also to the requirements of the universal common good, that is, of the international communities of different nature and scope. It is clear that
the standards of judgement set forth above are binding always and
everywhere, but the degree according to which concrete cases are
to be gauged cannot be established without reference to the available wealth; wealth which can vary in both quantity and quality,
which can, and in fact does, vary from country to country and
within the same country from time to time.

*Process of adjustment between economic development and social
progress*
          Whereas the economies of various countries are evolving ra-
pidly and at an even more intense pace during this post-war period, We consider it opportune to call attention to a fundamental
principle, namely that social progress accompany and be adjusted
to economic development so that all classes of citizens can participate in the increased productivity. Attentive vigilance and effective effort must be made so that socio-economic inequalities do
not increase but rather that they are lessened as much as possible.
"Likewise the national economy," observes Our Predecessor Pius
XII with evident justification, "as it is the product of the men who
work together in the community of the State, has no other end
than to secure without interruption the material conditions in
which the individual life of the citizen may fully develop. Where
this is secured in a permanent way, a people will be, in a true
sense, economically rich because the general well-being, and consequently the personal right of all to the use of worldly goods is thus
realised in conformity with the purpose willed by the Creator."
From this it follows that the economic wealth of a people arises
not only from an aggregate abundance of goods but also, and
more so, from their real and efficacious redistribution according to
justice, as a guarantee of the personal development of the members
of society, which is the true scope of a national economy. We must
here call attention to the fact that in many economies today, the
medium and large enterprises not rarely effect rapid and large
productive developments by means of self-financing. In such cases

We hold that the workers should acquire shares in the firms in which they are engaged, especially when they earn no more than the minimum salary. In this matter is to be recalled the principle explained by Our Predecessor Pius XI in the Encyclical *Quadragesimo Anno* : "It is totally false to ascribe to capital alone or to labour alone that which is obtained by the joint effort of the one and the other; and it is flagrantly unjust that either should deny the efficacy of the other and seize all the profits."

The demand of justice referred to can be satisfied in many ways suggested by experience. One of these, and, among the most desirable, is to see to it that the workers, in the manner and to a degree most convenient are able to participate in the ownership of the enterprise itself; since today more than in the times of Our Predecessor "every effort, therefore, must be made that at least in the future a just share only of the fruits of production be permitted to accumulate in the hands of the wealthy, and that an ample sufficiency be supplied to the working men."

But we should remember that adjustments between recompense for work and returns should be brought about in conformity with the demands of the common good both of one's own community and of the entire human family.

The demands of the common good on the national level must be considered : to provide employment to the greatest number of workers; to take care lest privileged classes arise, even among the workers; to maintain an equal balance between wages and prices, and make goods and services accessible to the greater number of citizens; to eliminate or keep within limits the inequalities between sectors of agriculture, of industry and of services; to bring about a balance between economic expansion and the development of essential public services; to adjust, as far as possible, the means of production to the progress of science and technology; to regulate the improvements in the tenor of life of the present generation with the objective of preparing a better future for the coming generations. There are also demands for the common good on the world level : to avoid all forms of unfair competition between the economies of different countries; to encourage with fruitful understanding collaboration among these national economies; to co-operate in the economic development of communities, economically less advanced. It is obvious that the demands of the common good, referred to both on the national and world level, are to be kept in mind when there is question of determining the rate of return to be asigned as profit to those responsible for the direction of the enterprise; also to the contributors of capital, in the form of interest and dividends.

THE DEMANDS OF JUSTICE IN REGARD TO THE PRODUCTIVE STRUCTURE IN HARMONY WITH MAN

Justice is to be observed not only in the distribution of wealth, but also with reference to the structures of the enterprises in which productive activity unfolds itself. There is, in fact, an innate exigency in human nature which demands that when men are engaged in productive activity, they have the opportunity of employing their own responsibility and perfecting their own being. Wherefore if the structures, the functioning, the surroundings of an economic system are such as to compromise human dignity, in so far as in them they unfold their proper activity, or if they systematically blunt in them the sense of responsibility, or constitute in any way an impediment to expressing their personal initiative, such an economic system is unjust, even if, by hypothesis, the wealth produced through it reaches a high standard and this wealth is distributed according to the criteria of justice and equity.

Confirmation of a directive

It is not possible to set out in detail that structure of an economic system which is more in conformity with the dignity of man and more suitable to developing in him a sense or responsibility. Nevertheless, Our Predecessor, Pius XII opportunely delineates this directive as follows : "the small and average sized undertakings in agriculture, in the arts and crafts, in commerce and industry, should be safeguarded and fostered by granting them the benefits of the larger firm by means of co-operative unions; while in the large concerns there should be the possibility of moderating the contract of work by one of partnership."

Artisan and Co-operative Enterprises

The artisan enterprise and the farm enterprise of family size, as also the co-operative enterprise that serves likewise as an element of integration of the two, are to be preserved and encouraged, in keeping with the common good and within the limits of technical possibilities. We shall return shortly to the topic of the farm enterprise of family size. Here, We think it appropriate to underscore the importance of the artisan and co-operative enterprises. Above all, it is necessary to emphasise that the two undertakings, in order to be effective, must constantly adapt themselves in their structure, function and output, to ever new situations, created by the advance of science and technology as also by the changing demands and preferences of the consumer. This adaptation must be first of all effected by the craftsmen themselves and the members themselves of the co-operative. To accomplish this, the two groups must have a good training, both technically and humanly, and they must be organised professionally. Further, it is imperative that appropriate economic measures be taken by the government regarding especially their information, taxation, credit and social security. Moreover, the measures taken by public agencies on behalf of the craftsmen and members of the co-operatives are justified by the fact that these two categories of citizens uphold true human values and contribute to the advance of civilisation. For these reasons, We paternally invite Our beloved sons, artisans and members of the co-operatives throughout the world, to realise the dignity of their profession and their substantial contribution, so that they keep alert the sense of responsibility and the spirit of co-operation in the national communities, and that the desire to work with dedication and originality ever abide.

Participation of workers in average-size large enterprises

Further, following up the line of thought drawn by Our Predecessors, We also hold as justifiable the desire of the employees to participate in the activity of the enterprises to which they belong as workers. It is not feasible to define *a priori* the manner and degrees of such participation, since the workers are the ones who are in touch with the specific conditions prevailing in every enterprise —conditions that can vary from one to another and are frequently subject to quick and substantial changes. But We think it fitting to call attention to the fact that the problem of the participation of the workers is an ever present one, whether the enterprise is private or public; at any rate, every effort should be made that the enterprise should be a community of persons in the dealings, activities and standing of all its members. This demands that the relations between the employers and directors on the one hand, and the employees on the other, be marked by appreciation, understanding, a loyal and active co-operation, and devotion to an undertaking common to both, and that the work be considered and effected by all the members of the enterprise, not merely as a source of income, but also as the fulfilment of a duty and the rendering of a service. This also means that the workers may have their say in, and may make their contribution to, the efficient running and development of the enterprise. Our Predecessor, Pius XII, remarked that " the economic and social function which every man aspires to fulfil, demands that the carrying on of the activity of each one is not completely subjected to the will of others." A humane view of the enterprise ought undoubtedly to safeguard the authority and necessary efficiency of the unity of direction, but it must not reduce its daily co-workers to the level of simple and silent performers without any possibility of bringing to bear their experience, keeping them entirely passive in regard to decisions that regulate their activity.

Finally, attention is to be called to the fact that the exercise of responsibility on the part of the workers in productive units, not only corresponds to the lawful demands inherent in human nature but is also in conformity with historical development in the economic, social and political fields. Unfortunately, as We have already noted, and as will later be seen more fully, numerous are the economic and social inequalities which in our time are opposed to justice and humanity; and deep rooted are the errors that pervade the activity, purposes, structure and working of the economic world. But it is and undeniable fact that the productive systems, thanks to the impulse deriving from scientific and technical advance, are today becoming more modern and efficient at a far more rapid rate than in the past. This demands of the workers greater abilities and professional qualifications. At the same time and as a consequence, they are given greater means and more free-time for being insructed and brought up to date, for acquiring culture and for their moral and religious formation. Thus can be provided also a longer period for basic instruction, as likewise for the professional training of new generations. Thus is created a humane environment that encourages the working classes to assume greater responsibility also within the enterprises, while at the same time political communities become ever more aware that all the citizens feel responsible for furthering the common good in all spheres of life.

The worker's participation at all levels

Modern times have seen a broad development of associations of workers and the general recognition of such in the juridical codes of various countries and on an international scale, for the specific purpose of co-operation, in particular by means of collective bargaining. But We cannot fail to emphasise how timely and imperative is it that the workers exert their influence, and effectively so, beyond the limits of the individual productive units, and at every level. The reason is that the individual productive units, regardless how extensive or how very efficient they are, form a vital part of the economic and social complexity of the respective political communities and are determined by it. Hence it is not the decisions made within the individual productive units which are those that have the greatest bearing, instead it is those made by public authorities or by institutions that act on a world-wide, regional or national scale, and pertaining to some economic sector or category of production. Hence the appropriateness or imperativeness that among such authorities or institutions, besides the holders of capital or the representatives of their interests, the workers also or those who represent their rights, demands and aspirations, should have a say. Our affectionate thought and Our paternal encouragement go out to the professional groups and to the associations of workers of Christian inspiration existing and working on more than one continent, which in the midst of many and frequently grave difficulties have been able and are continuing to strive for the effective promotion of the interests of the working classes and for their material and moral improvement, both within a single political unit as well as on a world-wide scale.

It is with satisfaction that We believe it Our duty to underscore the fact that their work is to be gauged not only by direct results and those immediately observable but also by the positive reaction of an economic and social order marked by justice and humanity, effected throughout the labour world, where it spreads the principles of correct orientation and supplies the impulse of Christian renovation. We believe further that such, too, ought to be considered the work performed with true Christian spirit by Our beloved sons in other professional groups and associations of workers just taking their inspiration from natural principles, in dealing with each other and respectful of freedom of conscience. We are also happy to express heartfelt appreciation to the International Labour Organisation which for decades has been making its ef fective and precious contribution to the establishment in the world of an economic and social order marked by justice and humanity, where also the lawful demands of the workers are given expression.

PRIVATE PROPERTY

Changed conditions

During these last decades, as is known, the difference has been growing more acute between the ownership of productive goods and the responsibility of those managing the larger economic entities. We know that this brings about problems hard to control by the public authorities in order to make certain that the aims pursued by the directors of large companies, especially of those that have greater effect on the entire economic life of a political community, are not contrary to the demands of the common good; problems, which as experience shows arise regardless whether the capital that makes possible the vast undertakings belong to private citizens or to public corporations.

It is also true that there are many citizens today—and their number is on the increase who through belonging to insurance groups or social security, have reason to face the future with serenity, a serenity that formerly derived from the properties they inherited, however modest. Finally, it is noted that today men strive to acquire professional training rather than become owners of property, and that they have greater confidence in income deriving from work or rights founded on work rather than in income deriving from capital or rights founded on capital. Moreover, this is in conformity with the pre-eminent position of work as the immediate expression of the individual against capital, a good by nature instrumental; and hence such a view of work may be considered a step forward in the process of human civilisation. The aspects just alluded to, which the economic world reveals, have certainly contributed in spreading the doubt that a principle of the economic and social order consistently taught by Our Predecessors has diminished or lost its importance, namely the principle of the natural right of private ownership inclusive of productive goods.

Confirmation of the right of ownership

There is no reason for such a doubt to persist. The right of private ownership of goods, including productive goods has a permanent validity, precisely because it is a natural right founded on the ontological and final priority of individual human beings as compared with society. Moreover, it would be useless to insist on free and personal initiative in the economic field, if the same initiative were not permitted to dispose freely of the means indispensable to its achievement. Further, history and experience testify that in those political regimes which do not recognise the rights of private ownership of goods, productive included, the fundamental manifestations of freedom are suppressed or stifled; hence one may justifiably conclude that they find in such a right both a guarantee and an incentive. Hence, is explained the fact that socio-political movements which strive to reconcile in society justice and liberty, were until recently clearly opposed to the private ownership of productive goods, but are now (more fully enlightened concerning actual social conditions) reconsidering their own stand and are taking in regard to that right an essentially positive attitude.

Accordingly, We make Our own the insistence of Our Predecessor Pius XII: "In defending the principle of private property the Church is striving after an important ethico-social end. She does not intend merely to uphold the present condition of things as if it were an expression of the Divine Will or to protect on principle the rich and plutocrats against the poor and indigent . . . The Church rather aims at securing that the institution of private property be such as it should be according to the plan of Divine Wisdom and the dispositions of Nature." And thus may the natural right be the guarantee of the essential freedom of the individual and at the same time an indispensable element in the social order. Further, We have observed today in many political communities, that economic systems are rapidly increasing their productive efficiency. With the increase of income, justice and fairness demand, as we have already seen, that remuneration for work be also increased within the limits allowed by the common good. This allows the workers more easily to save and thus acquire their own property. Hence, it is incomprehensible how the innate character of a right can be called into question that has as its main source the fruitfulness of work and is continually fostered by the same; a right that constitutes an apt means to assert one's personality and to exercise responsibility in every field; an element of solidity and of security for family life and of the peaceful and orderly development of society.

Effective distribution

It is not enough to assert the natural character of the right of private property, productive included, but the effective distribution among all social classes is to be insisted upon. As Our Predecessor Pius XII states : "Ordinarily, as a natural fundamental for living, the right to the use of the goods of the earth to which corresponds the fundamental obligation of granting private property to all if possible," while among the demands arising from the moral dignity of work, is also the one that includes "the conservation and perfection of a social order which makes possible a secure, even if modest property to all classes of the people. The distribution of property ought to be championed and effected in times such as ours, in which, as has been noted, the economic systems of an increasing number of political communities are in the process of rapid development. While making use of various technical devices which have proved effective, they find it easy to promote enterprises and carry out an economic and social policy that favours and facilitates an increased distribution of private ownership and of durable consumer goods, of homes, of farms, of one's own equipment in artisan enterprises and farms of family size, of shares in middle-sized and large firms—as is being profitably experienced in some political communities that have developed economically and progressed socially.

Public property

What has been set forth above, does not exclude, as is obvious, that the State also and other public agencies should lawfully possess as property productive goods especially when they "carry with them an opportunity too great to be left to private individuals without injury to the community at large." In modern times there is the tendency towards a progressive taking over of property whose ownership is vested in the State or other agencies of public authority The fact finds its explanation in the ever widening activity which the common good requires the public authorities to carry on. But also in the present matter the principle of subsidiarity stated above is to be followed. Accordingly, the State and the other agencies of public law should not extend their ownership except where motives of evident and real necessity of the common good require it, and not for the purpose of reducing and, much less, of abolishing private property. Nor is one to forget that the enterprises of an economic nature of the State and the other agencies of public law are to be entrusted to those who unite in themselves a specific solid ability, spotless honesty and keen sense of responsibility towards their country. Further, their behaviour and activity are to be subject to a wise and constant inspection, in order to preclude, among other things, that within the very organisation of the State should be formed centres of economic power that would operate to the detriment of its raison d'etre, that is the good of the community.

Social Function

Another doctrinal point constantly set forth by Our Predecessors is that with the right of private property is intrinsically linked a social function. As a matter of fact, according to the plan of creation, the goods of the earth are above all destined for the worthy support of all human beings, as Our Predecessor Leo XIII in his Encyclical *Rerum Novarum* expresses so wisely : "whoever has received from the Divine bounty a large share of blessings, whether they be external or corporal, or gifts of the mind, has received them for the purpose of using them for perfecting his own nature and, at the same time, that he may employ them, as the minister of God's Providence for the benefit of others. 'He that hath a talent' says St. Gregory the Great, 'let him see that he hideth it not; he that hath abundance, let him arouse himself to mercy and generosity; he that hath art and skill, let him do his best to share the use and utility thereof with his neighbour'." Today, the State as well as the agencies of public law have extended and are continuing to extend the sphere of their activity and initiative. But not for that reason has the raison d'etre of the social function of private property diminished, as some wrongly tend to believe; in as much as it derives from the very nature of the right of property. Further, there is always a wide range of tragic conditions and needs that demand tact, yet are nonetheless urgent, which the official means of public agencies cannot reach, or at any rate cannot assist. Hence there ever remains a vast sphere for the human sympathy and Christian charity of individuals.

Finally it has also been noted that frequently the numerous

efforts of individuals or of groups are much more effective in promoting spiritual values than the activity of public agencies. We should like to note at this point that in the Gospel the right of private ownership of goods is regarded as lawful. But at the same time, the Divine Master frequently extends to the rich the insistent invitation to convert their material goods into spiritual ones by conferring them on the needy — spiritual goods that the thief cannot steal nor the moth or rust destroy and which will be found increased in the eternal store houses of the Heavenly Father; "Lay not up to yourselves treasures on earth; where the rust and moth consume, and where thieves break through and steal. But lay up to yourselves treasures in heaven; where neither the rust nor moth doth consume, and where thieves do not break through, nor steal." And the Lord will consider as given or refused to Himself the charity given or refused to the needy, "as long as you did it to one of these my least brethren, you did it to me."

NEW ASPECTS OF THE SOCIAL QUESTION

The evolution of historical situations brings out into ever greater relief how the exigencies of justice and equity not only have a bearing on the relations between dependent working man and contractors or employers, but concern also the relations between different economic sectors and between areas economically more developed and those economically less developed within individual political communities; and, on the world plane, the relations between countries with a different degree of economic-social development.

Agriculture, a depressed sector

On the world plane it does not seem that the agricultural-rural population, in absolute terms, has decreased; but it is undeniable that an exodus of farm-rural peoples to urban agglomerations or centres is taking place—an exodus that is taking place in almost all countries and that sometimes assumes massive proportions, creating complex human problems difficult of solution. We know that as an economy develops, the number engaged in agriculture decreases, while the percentage of people employed in industry and in the area of services rises. Nevertheless, We think that the movement of the population from the farm area to other productive

M

sectors, besides the objective reasons of economic development, is often due to multiple factors, among which have been enumerated the desire to escape from surroundings considered as shut in and devoid of prospects; the longing for novelty and adventure that has taken hold of the present generation; the attraction of easily-gotten riches; the mirage of living in greater freedom, enjoying means and facilities that urban agglomerations and centres offer. But We also hold as beyond doubt that one of the forces behind this exodus is the fact that the farming sector, almost everywhere, is a depressed area, whether as regards the index of productivity, of population or as regards the standard of living of agricultural-rural populations. Thus, a fundamental problem that arises in practically all political communities is the following : how to proceed in order that the disproportion in productive efficiency between the agricultural sector on the one hand and, on the other, the industrial sector and that of services be reduced; that the standard of living of the farm-rural population be as close as possible to the standard of living of city people, who draw their resources from the industrial sector and from that of the service sector; that the tillers of the soil may not be possessed of an inferiority complex, but rather be persuaded that even in agriculture they can develop their personality through their toil and look forward to the future with confidence. It seems to Us opportune, therefore, to indicate certain directives that can contribute to a solution of the problem : directives which We believe have value whatever may be the historical environment in which one acts, on condition, obviously, that they may be applied in the manner and to the degree the surroundings allow or suggest or demand.

The equalisation of the essential public services
    It is above all indispensable that great care be taken, especially by the public authorities, to ensure that the essential services in country areas are suitably developed : good roads, transport, means of communication, drinking water, housing, health services, element-ary education and technical and professional training, conditions suitable for the practice of religion, means of recreation; and to ensure that there should be a good supply of those products which enable the country home to be well equipped and to be run on modern lines. Whenever such services, necessary today for a be-coming standard of living, are lacking in country areas, economic

development and social progress become almost impossible or develop too slowly; and the consequence of this is that the flow of population away from the country becomes almost impossible to check and difficult to control.

Gradual and Harmonious Development of the Economic System

It is also necessary that the economic development of the political communities should take effect in a gradual way and maintain a harmonious balance between all the sectors of production; that is to say, it is necesary that in cultivating the ground there should be put into practice innovations concerning methods of production, the choice of the type of agriculture and of the enterprise that the economic system considered as a whole allows or requires; and that they should be put into practice, as far as possible, in a degree proportioned to that carried out in the industrial service sector. In this way, agriculture absorbs a larger amount of industrial goods and demands a higher quality of services; in its turn, it offers to the other two fields and to the whole community the products which best meet, in quality and quantity, the needs of the consumer, contributing to the stability of the purchasing power of money, a very positive factor in the orderly development of the entire economic system. In such a way, We believe that it would also prove less difficult, both in areas which the population is leaving as well as in those to which they are flolcking, to control the movement of the labour force, set free by the progressive modernisation of agriculture; to provide them with the professional training as well as in those to which they are flocking, to control the production, and with the economic aid, preparation and spiritual assistance that will bring about their integration into society.

Appropriate economic policy

To obtain an economic development that preserves a harmonious balance among all the sectors of production, a prudent economic policy in the area of agriculture is also required; an economic policy that takes into account taxation, credit, social insurance, price protection, the fostering of integrating industries and the adjustment of the structures of enterprises.

Taxation

The fundamental principle in a system of taxation based on

justice and equity is that the burdens be proportioned to the capacity of the people contributing. But the common good also requires that in the assessment of tax, it must be borne in mind that, in the sector of agriculture, the returns develop more slowly and are exposed to greater risks in their production, and that there is greater difficulty in obtaining the capital necessary to increase them.

Capital at suitable interest

For the reasons mentioned above, the possessors of capital have little inclination to make investments in this sector; they are more inclined to invest in the other sectors instead. For the same reason agriculture cannot make a return of high interest nor even, as a rule, the trading profit to furnish the capital necessary for its own development and the normal exercise of its affairs. It is therefore necessary, for reasons of the common good, to evolve a special credit policy and to create credit institutes which will guarantee to agriculture such capital at a rate of interest on suitable terms.

Social Insurance and Social Security

In agriculture the existence of two forms of insurance may be indispensable; one concerned with the agricultural produce, the other with the farm workers and their families. Because the return per head is generally less in agriculture than in the sectors of industry and of services, it would not be in accordance with the standards of social justice and equity to set up systems of social insurance or of social security in which the allowances accorded to the forces of agricultural labour and of the individual families were substantially lower than those guaranteed to the sectors of industry and of services We consider that social policy must aim at guaranteeing that the insurance allowances made to the people should not be materially different no matter in what economic sector they work of the income on which they live. The systems of social insurance and social security can contribute efficaciously to a re-distribution of the overall income of the political community, according to the standards of justice and equity; and can therefore be considered as one of the instruments for restoring the balance in the standards of living in the different categories of the people.

Price Protection

Given the nature of agricultural produce, it is necessary that an effective system of regulation should be enforced to protect prices, making use, to this end, of the numerous expedients which present day economic technique can offer. It is very desirable that such regulation should be, primarily, the work of the interested parties; though supervision by the public authority cannot be dispensed with. On this subject it must not be forgotten that the price of agricultural produce represents rather the reward of labour than the remuneration of capital. Pope Pius XI in the Encyclical *Quadragesimo Anno* rightly observes that, "a reasonable relationship between different wages here enters into consideration," but He immediately adds, "Intimately connected with this is a reasonable relationship between the prices obtained for the products of the various economic groups : agrarian, industrial, etc." While it is true that farm produce is destined above all to satisfy the primary needs of man, and hence their price should be within the means of all consumers, still this cannot be used as an argument to keep a part of the citizens in a permanent state of economic and social inferiority by depriving them of the indispensable purchasing power in keeping with man's dignity. For this would be diametrically opposed to the common good.

Integration of farm income

It is also opportune to promote in agricultural regions the industries and services pertaining to the preservation, processing, and transportation of farm products. It is further desirable that in these regions undertakings in respect to other economic sectors and other professional activities be developed, so that farmers can augment their income in the surroundings where they live and work.

It is not possible to determine *a priori* what the structure of farm life should be because of the diversity of the rural conditions in each political community, not to mention the immense differences obtaining between the nations of the world. But if we hold to a human and Christian concept of man and the family, we are forced to consider as an ideal that community of persons operating on internal relations; whose structure is formed according to the demands of justice and the principles stated above, and still more, enterprises of family size. With these in mind we should exert every effort to realise one or the other, as far as circumstances permit.

But it is necessary to call attention to the fact that the enterprise of family size requires economic conditions which can ensure sufficient income to enable the family to live in decent comfort. To attain this end, it seems necessary not only that farmers be given up-to-date instructions on the latest methods of cultivation, and technically assisted in their profession, it is also indispensable that they form a flourishing system of co-operative undertakings, be organised professionally and participate in public life, not only in administrative institutions, but also in political movements.

Rural workers protagonists in their own betterment

We are of the opinion that rural workers must take active part in their own economic advancement, social progress and cultural betterment. They can easily see how noble is their work either because they live out their lives in the majestic temple of creation; or because their work often concerns the life of plants and animals, a life that is inexhaustible in its expression, inflexible in its laws, rich in allusions to God, the Creator and Provider; or because they produce food necessary to nourish the human family and furnish an increasing number of raw materials for industry. Furthermore, it is a work which carries with it the dignity of a calling which is marked by its manifold relationship with machines, chemistry and biology, relationships in continual development because of the repercussions of scientific and technical progress on the farm. It is also a work characterised by a moral dimension proper to itself, for it demands capacity for orientation and adaptation, patience in its many hours of waiting, sense of responsibility, spirit of perseverance and enterprise.

Solidarity and co-operation

We should like to recall to your minds also that in agriculture, as in other sectors of production, association is a vital need today, the more so as this sector has as its base the family size enterprise. Rural workers should feel a sense of solidarity one with another, and should unite to form co-operatives and professional associations, which are very necessary if they are to benefit from scientific and technical progress in methods of production, if they are to contribute in an efficacious manner to defend the prices of their products, if they are to attain an equal footing with other economical professional classes who are likewise usually organised. They need to organise to have a voice in political circles as well as in organs of public administration, for today almost nobody hears much less pays attention to isolated voices.

Awareness of the demands of the common good

However, rural workers (as workers in every other productive setcor), in using their various organisations must be governed by moral and juridical principles. They must try to reconcile their rights and interests with those of other classes of workers, and even subordinate one to the other if the common good demands it. The rural workers engaged in improving the condition of the whole agricultural world can legitimately demand that their efforts be seconded and complemented by the public authorities when they show themselves aware of the common good and contribute to its realisation. At this point, it is with pleasure We express Our satisfaction with Our sons in various parts of the world who are actively engaged in co-operatives, in professional groups and in worker movements, with a view to raising the economic and social standards of rural workers.

Vocation and mission

In the work on the farm the human personality finds numerous incentives for self-expression, for self-development, for enrichment, for growth, even in regard to spiritual values. Therefore, it is a work which is conceived and lived both as a vocation and as a mission. It can be considered as an answer to God's call to actuate His Providential plan in history. It may also be considered as a noble undertaking to elevate oneself and others and as a contribution to human civilisation.

Action to bring equality and to encourage the advancement of under-developed regions

Among citizens of the same political community there often exists marked economic and social inequality due for the most part to the fact that some live and work in areas that are economically more developed, while others live and work in areas that are economically under-developed. When this situation obtains, justice and equity demand that the public authorities should try to eliminate or reduce such inequality, to accomplish this end the public authorities should see to it that the under-developed areas be assured essential public services, which should be in the form and in the extent suggested or required by the surroundings and corresponding usually to the average standard of life that obtains in the national communities. Furthermore, it is necessary to develop a suitable economic and social policy regarding the supply of labour and the dislocation of population, wages, taxes, interest, investments, with special attention to expanding industries—in short a policy capable of promoting complete employment of the labour force, of stimulating enterprising initiative, and of exploiting the natural resources of the place. But governmental action along these lines must always be justified by the demands of the common good, which requires that all three areas of production, agriculture, industry and public services, be developed gradually simultaneously harmoniously to obtain unity on the national level. Special effort must be made that the citizens of the less developed regions take an active part, insofar as circumstances allow, in their economic betterment. Finally, it is necessary to remember that even private enterprise must contribute to an economic and social balance among among the different zones of the same country. And indeed public authorities, in accordance with the principle of sudsidiarity, must encourage and help private enterprise, entrusting to it, as far as efficiently possible, the continuation of economic development.

Elimination or reduction of unbalance between land and population.

It is not out of place to remark here that there are not a few countries where gross disproportion between land and population exists. In some countries there is scarcity of population, and tillable land abounds; in others, on the other hand, the population is large, while arable land is scarce. Furthermore, there are some countries where, in spite of rich natural resources, not enough food is produced to feed the population because of primitive methods of agriculture; on the other hand, in some countries, on account of modern methods of agriculture, food surpluses have become an economic problem. It is obvious that the solidarity of the human race and Christian brotherhood demand that among the peoples of the world active and manifold co-operation be established, co-operation which permits and encourages the movement of goods, capital and men, with a view to eliminate or reduce the above-mentioned unbalance. Later on, We shall treat this point in more detail. Here, however, We should like to express Our sincere appreciation for the highly beneficial work which the United Nations' Food and Agricultural Organisation (FAO) is undertaking to establish fruitful accord among nations, to promote the modernisation of agriculture especially in countries in the process of development, to alleviate the suffering of hunger-stricken peoples.

DEMANDS OF JUSTICE IN THE RELATIONSHIP BETWEEN NATIONS DIFFERING IN ECONOMIC DEVELOPMENT

The problem of the modern world
Probably the most difficult problem of the modern world concerns the relationship between political communities that are economically advanced and those in the process of development. The standard of living is high in the former, while in the latter countries poverty, and, in some cases, extreme poverty exists. The solidarity which binds all men and makes them members of the same family imposes upon political communities enjoying abundance of goods the duty not to remain indifferent to those political communities whose citizens suffer from poverty, misery and hunger, and who lack even the elementary rights of the human person. This is the more so since, given the growing interdependence among the peoples of the earth, it is not possible to preserve lasting peace, if glaring economic and social inequality among them persists. Mindful of Our role of universal Father, We feel obliged solemnly to stress what We have in another connection stated : "We are all equally responsible for the undernourished peoples . . . Therefore, it is necessary to educate one's conscience to the sense of responsibility which weighs upon each and everyone, especially upon those who are more blessed with this world's goods."

It is obvious that the obligation, which the Church has always taught, to help those who find themselves in want and misery, should be felt more strongly by Catholics, who find a most noble motive in the fact that we are all members of Christ's Mystical Body. John, the Apostle, said : "In this we have known the charity of God, because he hath laid down his life for us : and we ought to lay down our lives for the brethren. He that hath the substance of this world, and shall see his brother in need, and shall shut up his bowels from him : how doth the charity of God abide in him?"

We, therefore, see with satisfaction that those political communities which enjoy high economic standards are providing assistance to political communities in the process of economic development in order that they may succeed in raising their standards of living.

Emergency assistance

There are countries which produce consumer goods and especially farm products in excess, while in other countries large segments of the population suffer from misery and hunger. Justice and humanity demand that the former come to the aid of the latter. To destroy or to squander goods that other people need in order to live, is to offend against justice and humanity. While it is true that to produce goods, especially agricultural products in excess of the needs of the political community can cause economic harm to a certain portion of the population, this is not a motive for exonerating oneself from the obligation of extending emergency aid to the indigent and hungry. Rather, all ingenuity should be used to contain the negative effects deriving from surplus goods, or at least to make the entire population equally share the burden.

Scientific, technical, and financial co-operation

Emergency aid, although a duty imposed by humanity and justice, is not adequate to eliminate or even to reduce the causes which in not a few political communities bring about a permanent state of want, misery and hunger. These causes flow, for the most part from the primitiveness or backwardness of their economic systems. And this cannot be remedied except by means of varied forms of co-operation directed to making these citizens acquire new outlooks, professional qualifications, and scientific and technical competence. This co-operation must also consists in putting at their disposal the necessary capital to start and to speed up their economic development with the help of modern methods. We are well aware that in these recent years the realisation has grown and matured that efforts should be made to favour the economic development and social progress of the countries which face the greatest difficulties. World and regional organisations, individual States, foundations and private societies offer to the above mentioned countries, in an increasing decree, their own technical co-operation in all productive spheres; and they multiply for thousands of young people facilities to study in the universities of the more developed countries and to acquire an up-to-date scientific, technical, and professional formation; while world banking institutes, single States and private persons furnish capital and give life, or help to give life, to an ever richer network of economic enterprises in the countries on the way to development. We are happy to profit by the present occasion to express Our sincere appreciation of such richly fruitful works. But We cannot excuse Ourselves from pointing out that the scientific, technical, and economic co-operation between the economically developed political communities and those just beginning or on the way to development needs to be increased beyond the present level; and it is Our hope that such a development will characterise their dealings during the next decades. On this matter We consider some reflections and warnings opportune.

Avoiding the errors of the past

Wisdom demands that the political communities that find themselves in the initial stage or little advanced in their economic development keep before their eyes the actual experiences of the already developed political communities. More and better production corresponds to a rational need and is also an absolute necessity. However, it is no less necessary and conformable to justice that the riches produced come to be evenly distributed among all members of the political community; hence efforts should be made that social progress proceed at the same pace as economic development. This means that it be advanced, as far as possible, gradually and harmoniously in all productive sectors, in those of agriculture, industry and services.

Respect for the characteristics of the individual communities

The political communities on the way towards economic development generally present their own unmistakable individuality, due either to their resources and the specific character of their own natural environment, or due to their traditions frequently abounding in human values, or due to the typical quality of their own members. The economically developed political communities when lending their help must recognize and respect this individuality and overcome the temptation to impose themselves by means of these works upon the community in the course of economic development.

Disinterested work

But the bigger temptation with which the economically developed political communities have to struggle is that of profiting from their technical and financial co-operation so as to influence the political situation of the less developed countries with a view to bringing about plans of world domination. If this takes place, it must be explicitly declared that it would be a new form of colonialism. which, however clearly disguised, would not tor all that be less blameworthy than that from which many peoples have recently escaped, and which would influence negatively their international relations, constituting a menace and danger to world peace. And it is, therefore, indispensable and corresponds to the need of justice that the above mentioned technical and financial aid be given in sincere political disinterestedness, for the purpose of putting those communities on the way to economic development, in a position to realise their own proper economic and social growth. In such a way, a precious contribution to the formation of a world community can be made, a community in which all members are subjects conscious of their own duties and rights, working on a basis of equality for the bringing about of the universal common good.

Respect for the hierarchy of values

Scientific and technical progress, economic development, the betterment of living conditions, are certainly positive elements in a civilisation. But we must remember that they are not nor can they be considered the supreme values, in comparison with which values they are seen as essentially instrumental in character. It is with sadness that We point out that in the economically developed countries there are not a few persons in whom the consciousness of the hierarchy of values is weakened, is dead, or confused; that is, in whom the spiritual values are neglected, forgotten, denied; while the progress of the sciences of technology, the economic development, the material well-being are often fostered and proposed as the pre-eminent, and even elevated to the unique, reasons of life. This constitutes an insidious poison, and one of the most dangerous, in the work which the economically developed peoples can give to those on the way to development : people in whom ancient tradition has quite often preserved a living and operating consciousness of some of the most important human values. To undermine this consciousness is essentially immoral. One must respect it and, where possible, clarify and develop it so that it will remain what it is : a foundation of true civilisation.

The contribution of the Church

The Church, as is known, is by divine right universal, and she is this also historically, from the fact that she is present or strives to be so among all peoples. The entrance of the Church among a people has always brought positive reactions in the social and economic fields, as history and experience show. The reason is that people on becoming Christian cannot but feel obliged to improve the institutions and the environment in the temporal order : whether to prevent these doing harm to the dignity of man or to eliminate or reduce the obstacles to the good and multiply the incentives and invitations to it. Moreover, the Church, entering the life of the people, is not nor does she consider herself to be an institution which is imposed from outside. This is due to the fact that her presence is brought about by the re-birth or resurrection of each person in Christ; and he who is re-born or rises again in Christ never feels himself constrained from without; indeed, he feels himself liberated in the deepest part of his being and thus open towards God; and whatever in him is of worth, whatever be its nature, is re-affirmed and ennobled. "The Church of Jesus Christ," as Our Predecessor Pius XII wisely observes, "is the repository of His wisdom; she is certainly too wise to discourage or belittle those peculiarities and differences which mark out one nation from another. It is quite legitimate for nations to treat those differences as a sacred inheritance and guard them at all costs. The Church aims at unity, a unity determined and kept alive by that supernatural love which should be actuating everybody; she does not aim at a uniformity which would only be external in its effects and would cramp the natural tendencies of the nations concerned. Every nation has its own genius, its own qualities, springing from the hidden roots of its being. The wise development, the encouragement within limits, of that genius, those qualities, does no harm; and if a nation cares to take precautions, to lay down rules, for that end, it has the Church's approval. She is mother enough to befriend such projects with her prayers." We notice with profound satisfaction how today also, the Catholic citizens of the countries moving towards economic development are not, as a rule, second to any in taking their part in the effort which their own countries are making to develop and raise themselves in the economic and social fields. Furthermore, Catholic citizens of the economically developed countries multiply efforts to help and make more fruitful the work being done for the communities still developing economically. Worthy of special consideration is the varied assistance that they increasingly give to students from the countries of Africa and Asia who are scattered throughout the universities of Europe and America; and the preparation of persons trained to go to the less developed countries in order to engage in technical and professional activity. To these Our beloved sons who in every continent show forth the perennial vitality of the Church in promoting genuine progress and in giving life to civilisation, We wish to join Our kind and paternal word of appreciation and encouragement.

POPULATION INCREASE AND ECONOMIC DEVELOPMENT

Lack of balance between population and means of sustenance

In recent years, the problem concerning the relationship between the population increase, economic development and the availability of the means of sustenance, whether on a world plane or as it confronts the economically developing political communities is very much to the fore again. On a worldwide scale, some observe that according to sufficiently reliable statistics, in a few decades the human family will reach a very high figure, while economic development will proceed at a slower rate. From this, they deduce that, if nothing is done in time to check the population flow, the lack of balance between the population and the food supply in the not too distant future will make itself felt acutely. In so far as this affects the political communities which are developing economically, still relying on statistical data, it is clear

that the rapid spread of hygienic measures and of appropriate me-
dical remedies will greatly reduce the death rate, especially among
infants; while the birth rate, which in some countries is usually
high, tends to remain more or less constant, at least for a considerable period of time. Therefore, the excess of births over deaths
will notably increase, while the productive efficiency of the respective economic systems will not increase proportionately. Accordingly, an improvement in the standards of living in these developing political communities is impossible; indeed it is inevitable
that things will get worse. Hence, to avoid a situation which will
result in extreme hardship, there are those who would have recourse to drastic measures of birth control or prevention.

The terms of the problem
To tell the truth, considered on a world scale, the relationship
between the population increase on the one hand and the economic development and availability of food supplies on the other,
does not seem—at least for the moment and in the near future
—to create a difficulty; in every case the elements from which one
can draw sure conclusions are too uncertain and changeable. Besides, God in His goodness and wisdom has diffused in nature inexhaustible resources and has given to man intelligence and genius
to create fit instruments to master it and to turn it to satisfy the
needs and demands of life. Hence, the real solution of the problem
is not to be found in expedients that offend against the moral
order established by God and which injure the very origin of human life, but in a renewed scientific and technical effort on the
part of man to deepen and extend his dominion over nature. The
progress of science and technology, already achieved, opens up in
this direction limitless horizons. We realise that in certain areas
and in the political communities of developing economies really
serious problems and difficulties can and do present themselves,
due to a deficient economic and social organisation which does
not offer, therefore, living conditions proportionate to the rate of
population increase; As also to the fact that the solidarity among
the people is not operative to a sufficient degree. But even in such
an hypothesis, We must immediately and clearly state that these
problems must not be confronted and these difficulties are not to be
overcome by having recourse to methods and means which are
unworthy of man and which find their explanation only in an

utterly materialistic concept of man himself and of his life. The true solution is found only in the economic development and in the social progress which respects and promotes the true human values, individual and social; an economic development and social progress, that is, brought about in a moral atmosphere, conformable to the dignity of man and to the immense value the life of a single human being has; and in the co-operation, on a world scale, that permits and favours an ordered and fruitful interchange of useful knowledge, of capital and of manpower.

Respect for the laws of life

We must solemnly proclaim that human life is transmitted by means of the family, the family founded on marriage, one and indissoluble, raised for Christians to the dignity of a Sacrament. The transmission of human life is entrusted by nature to a personal and conscious act and, as such, subject to the all-wise laws of God.; laws inviolable and immutable that are to be recognised and observed. Therefore, it is not permissible to use means and follow methods that can be licit for the transmission of plant or animal life. Human life is sacred; from its very inception, the creative action of God is directly operative. By violating His laws, the Divine Majesty is offended, the individuals themselves, and humanity degraded, and likewise the community itself of which they are members is enfeebled.

Education towards a sense of responsibility

It is of the greatest importance that the new generations be brought up with adequate cultural as well as religious formation, as is the duty and right of parents, leading to a profound sense of responsibility in all the expressions of their life and therefore also in regard to the forming of a family and to the procreation and education of the children. These ought to be formed in a life of faith and great trust in Divine Providence, in order to be ready to undergo fatigues and sacrifices in the fulfilment of a mission so noble and often arduous, as is the co-operation with God in the transmission of human life and the education of the offspring. For such education no institution provides so many efficacious resources as the Church which for this reason alone, has the right to full liberty to fulfil her mission.

In the service of life

Genesis relates how God imposed on the first human beings two commands : that of transmitting life; "Increase and multiply" and that of dominating nature; "Fill the earth and subdue it," commands which complement each other. Certainly the Divine command to dominate nature is not aimed at destructive purposes; instead it is for the service of life. We point out with sadness one of the most disturbing contradictions by which our epoch is tormented and by which it is being consumed, namely that, while on the one hand are brought out in strong relief situations of want, and the spectre of misery and hunger haunts us; on the other hand scientific discoveries, technical inventions and economic resources are being used, often extensively, to provide terrible instruments of ruin and death. A provident God grants sufficient means to the human race to solve in dignified fashion even the many and delicate problems attendant upon the transmission of life; but these problems can become difficult of solution or even insoluble because man, led astray in mind or perverted in will, turns to such means as are opposed to reason and hence he seeks ends that do not answer to man's social nature nor to the intentions of Providence.

CO-OPERATION ON A WORLD SCALE

World dimensions of every important human problem

The progress of science and technology in all aspects of life multiply and increase the relationships between political communities and hence render their interdependence ever more profound and vital. As a result, it can be said that most problems of importance, whatever their content be, scientific, technical, economic, social, political or cultural, present today supranational and often world wide dimensions. Hence, the different political communities can no longer adequately solve their major problems in their own surroundings and with their own forces, even though they be communities which are notable for the high level and diffusion of their culture, for the number and industriousness of their citizens, for the efficiency of their economic systems, and the vastness and the richness of their territories. Political communities react on each other; and it may be said that each succeeds in developing

N

itself by contributing to the development of the other. Hence, understanding and co-operation are so necessary.

Mutual Distrust

One can thus understand how in the minds of individual human beings and among different peoples the conviction of the urgent necessity of mutual understanding and co-operation is becoming ever more widespread. But at the same time, it seems that men, especially those entrusted with greater responsibility, show themselves unable to understand one another. The root of such inability is not to be sought in scientific, technical or economic reasons but in the absence of mutual trust. Men, and consequently States, fear each other. Each fears that the other harbours plans of conquest, and is waiting for the favourable moment to put these plans into effect. Hence, each organises its own defence and arms itself not for aggression, so it is said, but to deter the potential aggressor against any effective invasion. As a consequence, vast human energies and gigantic resources are employed in non-constructive purposes; meanwhile, in the minds of individual human beings and among peoples, a sense of uneasiness and reluctance which lessens the spirit of initiative for works on a broad scale arises and grows.

Failure to acknowledge the Moral Order

The lack of reciprocal trust finds its explanation in the fact that men, especially those more responsible, are inspired in the unfolding of their activity by different or radically opposed concepts of life. Unfortunately, in some of these concepts, the existence of the moral order is not recognised : an order which is transcendent, universal, absolute, equal and binding on all. Thus, they fail to meet and understand each other fully and openly in the light of one and the same law of justice admitted and adhered to by all. It is true that the term "justice" and the phrase, "demands of justice" are uttered by the lips of all. However, these utterances take on different and opposite meanings. Wherefore, the repeated and impassioned appeals to justice and the demands of justice, instead of offering the possibility of meeting or of understanding, increase the confusion, sharpen the contrasts, keep disputes inflamed. In consequence, the belief is spread that to enforce one's

rights and pursue one's own interests, no others means are left than
recourse to violence, font of the most serious evils.

The true God, foundation of the moral order
    Mutual trust among men and among States cannot begin
nor increase except by the recognition of and respect for the moral order. The moral order does not hold except in God; cut off
from God, it disintegrates. Man, in fact, is not only a material
organism but is also a spirit endowed with thought and freedom.
He demands, therefore, a moral and religious order, which bears
more than any material value on the directions and solution it
can give to the problems of individual and group life within the
national communities and the relationships among them. It has
been claimed that in an era of scientific and technical triumphs,
men can construct their civilisation without God. But the truth is
that these same scientific and technical advances present human
problems of a world-wide scope which can be solved only in the
light of a sincere and active faith in God, the beginning and end
of man in the world.
    These truths are confirmed by the ascertainment that the same
limitless horizons opened up by scientific research help to give birth
to the conviction and develop it that mathematical and scientific
notions point out but do not reach and much less express entirely
the more profound aspects of reality. The tragic experience that
the gigantic forces placed at the disposal of technology can be
used for purposes both constructive and destructive, makes evident
the pressing importance of spiritual values so that scientific and
technical progress may preserve its essentially instrumental character with reference to civilisation.
    Further, the sense of increasing this satisfaction which spreads
among human beings in the national communities of a high standard of living destroys the illusion of a hoped-for paradise on earth;
but at the same time, the consciousness of inviolable and universal
rights becomes ever clearer and ever more more forceful the aspir-
ation for juster and more human relations. These are all motives
which contribute toward making human beings more conscious of
their own limitations and toward creating in them a striving
for spiritual values; and this cannot be but a happy earnest of a
sincere understanding and profitable co-operation.

RECONSTRUCTION OF SOCIAL RELATIONSHIPS IN TRUTH, JUSTICE, AND LOVE

Incomplete and erroneous ideologies

After all this scientific and technical progress, and even because of it, there remains a problem how social relationships can be reconstructed in a more human balance both in regard to individual political communities and on a world scale. In the modern era, different ideologies have been devised and spread abroad with this in mind : some have been dissolved as clouds by the sun, others have undergone or are undergoing substantial changes; others have waned, faded away and are loosing still more their attraction on the minds of men. The reason is that they are ideologies which consider only certain and less profound aspects of man. And this because they do not take in to consideration certain inevitable human imperfections, such as sickness, and suffering, imperfections which even the most advanced economico-social systems cannot eliminate. Then there is the profound and imperishable religious need which constantly expresses itself everywhere, even though trampled down by violence or skilfully smothered. In fact the most fundamental modern error is that of considering the religious demands of the human soul as an expression of feeling or of fantasy, or a product of some contingent event which should be thus eliminated as an anachronism and as an obstacle to human progress; whereas by this craving human beings reveal themselves for what they really are; beings created by God, and for God, as St. Augustine cries out : "Thou hast made us for Thee, O Lord, and our heart is restless until it rests in Thee." Moreover, whatever the technical and economic progress, there will be neither justice nor peace in this world until men return to a sense of the dignity of creatures and sons of God. The just and final reason of of the being of all reality created by Him. Man separated from God becomes inhuman to himself and to those of his kind, because the orderly relation of society presupposes the orderly relation of one's conscience with God. Font of truth, of justice and of love.

It is true that the persecution of so many of Our dearly beloved brothers and sons, which has been raging for decades in many countries, even those of an ancient Christian civilisation, makes even clearer to Us the dignified superiority of the persecuted

and the refined barbarity of the persecutors; so that, if it does not
bring visible signs of repentance, it induces many to think. But it
is always true that the most perniciously typical aspect of the modern era consists in the absurd attempt to reconstruct a solid and
fruitful temporal order divorced from God, the only foundation
on which it can endure, and to want to celebrate the greatness of
man by drying up the font from which that greatness springs,
and from which it is nourished and hence restraining, and if possible, extinguishing man's sighing for God. Every day experience
continues to witness to the fact, amidst most bitter delusions and
not rarely in terms of blood, that, as stated in the inspired Book :
"Unless the Lord build the house, they labour in vain that build
it."

Perennial Actuality of the Social Doctrine of the Church
      The Church is the standard-bearer and herald of a way of
life which is ever up to date. The fundamental principle in such
a conception is, as is seen from what has thus far been said, that
individual human beings are and should be the foundation, the
end and the subjects of all the institutions in which social life
is carried on : individual human souls considered in so far as they
are and should be by their nature intrinsically social and in so far
as they are in the plan of Providence, by their elevation to the supernatural order. From this fundamental principle which guarantees the sacred dignity of the individual, the teaching office of the
Church has made clear, with the co-operation of enlightened
priests and laymen, especially during this last century, a social doctrine which points out with clarity the sure way to reconstruct all
social relationships according to universal criteria based on human nature and the various dimensions of the temporal order and
the characteristics of contemporary society and hence acceptable
to all. But it is indispensable, today more than ever, that this
doctrine be known, assimilated, and translated into social reality
in the form and manner that the different situations allow and demand; a most difficult task but a most noble one to the carrying
out of which We most warmly invite not only Our brothers and
sons scattered throughout the world but also all men of good will.

Instruction
      We re-affirm strongly that this Christian social doctrine is

an integral part of the Christian conception of life. While We note with satisfaction that in several Institutes this doctrine has been taught for some time, We feel urged to exhort that such teaching be exended by regular systematic courses in Catholic schools of every kind, especially in Seminaries. It is to be inserted into the religious instruction programmes of parishes and of Associations of the Lay Apostolate. It should be spread by every modern means of expression, daily newspapers and periodicals, publications of both a scientific and a popular nature, radio and television. To this diffusion Our beloved sons, the Laity, can greatly contribute by knowing this doctrine and making their actions conform to it, by zealously striving to make others understand it. They should be convinced that the truth and efficacy of this teaching is most easily demonstrated when they can show that it offers a safe part for the solution of present day difficulties. In this way they bring it to the attention of those who are opposed to it because they are ignorant of it; they may even cause a ray of light to enter into their minds.

Education

   A social doctrine has to be translated into reality and not just merely formulated. This is particularly true of the Christian social doctrine whose light is Truth, its objective Justice, and its driving force Love. Hence We stress the fact that it is of the greatest importance that Our beloved sons not only know this social doctrine but that they be educated according to it. Christian education should be complete, in extending itself to every kind of obligation, hence it should strive to implant and foster among the faithful an awareness of the obligation to carry on in a Christian manner their economic and social activites. The transition from theory to practice is of its very nature difficult; and is especially so when one tries to reduce to concrete terms a social doctrine such as that of the Church, on account of the deep rooted selfishness of human beings, the materialism in which modern society is steeped, and the difficulty of singling out precisely the demands of justice in particular cases. Consequently it is not enough for this education that men be taught their social obligations, they must also be given by practical action the methods that will enable them to fulfil these duties.

A Task for Association of the Apostolate of the Laity

Education to act in a Christian manner in economic and social matters will hardly succeed unless those being educated play an active role in their own formation, and unless the education is also carried on through action. Just as one cannot acquire the right use of liberty except by using liberty correctly, so one learns Christian behaviour in social and economic matters by actual Christian action in those fields. Hence, in social education Associations and Organisations of the Lay Apostolate play an important role, especially those that have as their specific objective the Christianisation of the economic and social sectors of the temporal order. Indeed, many members of these Associations can draw profit from their daily experiences to form themselves more completely and also to contribute to the social education of youth. At this point it seems opportune to recall to all, the great and the lowly, the Christian concept of life which requires a spirit of moderation and of sacrifice. Unfortunately, there is everywhere prevalent a hedonistic conception and tendency which would reduce life to the search after pleasure and the full satisfaction of all the passions, with a consequent great loss to both body and soul. On the natural level, simplicity of life and temperance in the lower appetites is a wisdom productive of good; on the supernatural level, the Gospels and the whole ascetic tradition of the Church require a sense of mortification and of penance which assures the rule of the spirit over the flesh and offers an efficacious means of expiating the punishment due to sin from which no one, except Jesus Christ and His Immaculate Mother, is exempt.

Practical suggestions

In reducing social principles and directives to practice, one usually goes through three stages : reviewing the situation, judging it in the light of these principles and directives, deciding what can and what should be done according to the mode and degree permitted by the situation itself. These are the three stages that are usually expressed in the three terms : look, judge, act. It is particularly important that youth be made to dwell often on these three stages and as far as possible reduce them to action. The knowledge acquired in this way does not remain merely abstract ideas but is something to be translated into deed. In the application of doctrine there can arise even among upright and sincere Catholics differences of opinion. When this happens, they should be watchful to keep alive mutual esteem and respect and should strive to find points of agreement for efficacious and suitable action. They should not exhaust themselves in interminable discussions and, under pretext of the better or the best, omit to do the good that is possible, and thus obligatory.

Catholics in their economic-social activities often find themselves in close contact with others who do not share their view of life. In these circumstances, Our sons should be very careful that they are consistent and never make compromises on religion and morals. At the same time let them show themselves animatd by a spirit of understanding and disinterestedness, ready to co-operate loyally in achieving objects that of their nature are good or at least reduceable to good. It is clear, however, that when the Hierarchy has made a decision on the point at issue, Catholics are bound to obey their directives because the Church has the right and obligation not merely to guard ethicol and religious principles, but also to intervene authoritatively in the temporal sphere when it is a matter of judging the application of these principles to concrete cases.

Manifold action and responsibility

From instruction and education one must pass to action. This is a task that belongs particularly to Our sons, the Laity, since, in virtue of their condition of life, they are constantly engaged in activities and in the formation of institutions that in their ends are temporal. In performing such a noble task, it is essential that Our sons be professionally qualified and carry on their occupation in conformity with its own proper laws in order to secure effectively the desired ends. It is equally necessary, however, that they act within the framework of the principles and directives of Christian social teaching and in an attitude of loyal trust and filial obedience to ecclesiastical authority. Let them remember that, when in the transaction of temporal affairs, they do not follow the principles and directives of Christian teaching, not only do they fail in their obligations and often violate the rights of their brethren, but they can also bring into discredit that very doctrine which, in spite of its intrinsic value, seems to be lacking in a truly directive power.

A grave danger

As We have already noted, modern man has greatly deepened
and extended his knowledge of the laws of nature and has made
instruments that make him lord of their forces; he has ever produced gigantic and spectacular works. Nevertheless, in his striving
to master and transform the external world, he is in danger of
forgetting and of destroying himself. As Pope Pius XI, Our Predecessor, observes with deep sadness in the Encyclical *Quadragesimo Anno* : "And so bodily labour, which was decreed by Providence for the good of man's body and soul even after original sin,
has everywhere been changed into an instrument of strange per-
version : for dead matter leaves the factory ennobled and trans-
formed, where men are corrupted and degraded." In a similar
manner Pope Pius XII, Our Predecessor, rightly asserted that our
age is marked by a clear contrast between the immense scientific
and technical progress and the fearful human decline shown by
"its monstrous masterpiece" of "transforming man into a giant of
the physical world at the expense of his spirit, which is reduced
to that of a pigmy in the supernatural and eternal world." Once
again is verified today, in a most striking manner, that which was
asserted of the pagans by the Psalmist, men forget their own being
in their works and admire their productions to the point of idolatry;
"the idols of the gentiles are silver and gold, the works of the hands
of men."

Recognition of and Respect for the Hierarchy of Values

In Our paternal care as universal Pastor of souls, We urgently
invite Our sons to take care that they keep alive and active an
awareness of a hierarchy of values as they carry on their temporal
affairs and seek their immediate ends. Certainly, the Church has
taught and always teaches that scientific and technical progress
and the resultant material well-being are truly good and, as such,
mark an important phase in human cvilisation. Nevertheless, these
things should be valued according to their true worth, namely, as
instruments or means used to achieve more effectively a higher end,
that of facilitating and promoting the spiritual perfection of mankind, both in the natural and the supernatural order. We desire
that the warning words of the Divine Master should ever sound
in the ears of men : "For what does it profit a man if he gained

the whole world and suffer the loss of his own soul? Or what exchange shall a man give for his soul?"

Sanctification of Sundays

To safeguard the dignity of man as a creature endowed with
a soul formed to the image and likeness of God, the Church has
always demanded an exact observance of the third precept of the
Decalogue : "Remember that thou keep holy the sabbath day." God
has a right to demand of man that he dedicate a day of the week
to worship, in which the spirit, free from material preoccupations,
can lift itself up and open itself by thought and by love to heavenly
things, examining in the secret of its conscience its obligatory and
necessary relations towards its Creator. In addition, man has the
right as well as the need to rest in order to renew the bodily
strength used up by hard daily work, to give suitable recreation
to the senses and to promote domestic unity, which requires frequent contact and a peaceful living together of all the members of
the family. Consequently, religion, morality and hygiene, all unite
in the law of periodic repose which the Church has for centuries
translated into the sanctification of Sunday through participation
in the Holy Sacrifice of the Mass, a memorial and application of
the redemptive work of Christ for souls.

It is with great grief that We must acknowledge and deplore
the negligence of, if not the downright disrespect for, this sacred
law and the consequent harmful results for the health of both
body and soul of Our beloved workers. In the name of God and
for the material and spiritual interests of men, We call upon all,
public authorities, employers and workers, to observe the precepts
of God and of His Church, and We remind each one of his grave
responsibilities before God and society.

Renewed obligation

In what We have briefly exposed above, it would be an error
if Our sons, especially the Laity, should consider it more prudent
to lessen the personal Christian commitment in the world; rather
should they renew and increase it. Our Lord, in the sublime prayer
for the unity of the Church, did not ask the Father to take His
own from the world but to preserve them from evil :"I pray not
that Thou shouldst take them out of the world, but that Thou
shouldst keep them from evil." We should not create an artificial

opposition between the perfection of one's own being and one's
personal active presence in the world; as if a man could not perfect himself except by putting aside all temporal activity, and that
whenever such action is done, a man is inevitably led to compromise his personal dignity as a human being and as a believer. Instead of this being so, it is perfectly in keeping with the plan of
Divine Providence that each one develop and perfect himself
through his daily work, which for almost all human beings is of
a temporal nature. Today, the Church is confronted with the immense task of giving a human and Christian note to modern civilisation; a note that is required and almost asked by that civilisation itself for its future development and even for its continued
existence. As We have already emphasised, the Church fufils this
mission through her lay sons who should thus feel pledged to carry
on their professional activities as the fulfilment of a duty, as the
performance of a service in the internal union with God and with
Christ and for His glory, as St. Paul points out : "Whether you
eat or drink, or whatsoever else you do, do all for the glory of
God," "all whatsoever you do in word or in work, do all in the
name of the Lord Jesus Christ, giving thanks to God and the Father by Him."

Greater efficiency in temporal affairs

In temporal affairs and institutions, whenever an awareness
of values and supernatural ends is secured, there is at the same
time a strengthening of their power to achieve their immediate
specific ends. The words of our Divine Master are still true : "Seek
ye, therefore, first the kingdom of God and His justice; and all
these things shall be added unto you." When it is "now light in
the Lord" and one walks as "children of the light," the fundamental demands of justice are more securely grasped in the most difficult and complex regions of temporal affairs, namely those in
which selfishness, individual, group or racial, often causes thick
clouds of darkness. When one is animated by the charity of Christ
one feels united to others, and the needs, suffering and joys of
others are felt as one's own. Consequently, the action of each one,
no matter what the object or circumstances in which it may be
realised, cannot help being more disinterested, more energetic, more
human, because charity "is patient, is kind... seeketh not her own...

rejoiceth not in iniquity, but rejoiceth with the truth... hopeth all things, endureth all things."

Living members in the Mystical Body of Christ
We cannot conclude Our Encyclical without recalling another sublime truth and reality, namely that we are living members of the Mystical Body of Christ, which is His Church : "For as the body is one and hath many members; and all the members of the body, whereas they are many, yet are one body : so also is Christ." We invite with paternal urgency all Our sons belonging to either the Clergy or the Laity to be deeply conscious of this dignity and nobility due to the fact that they are grafted on to Christ as shoots on a vine; "I am the vine and you are the branches"; and they are thus called to live by His very life. Hence, when one carries on one's proper activity, even if it be of temporal nature, in union with Jesus, the Divine Redeemer, every work becomes a continuation of His work and penetrated with redemptive power : "He that abideth in me, and I in him, the same beareth much fruit." It thus becomes a work which contributes to one's personal supernatural perfection and helps to extend to others the fruits of the redemption and leavens with the ferment of the Gospel the civilisation in which one lives and works. Our era is penetrated and shot through by radical errors, it is torn and upset by deep disorders. Nevertheless, it is also an era in which immense possibilities for good are opened to the Church.

Beloved brethren and sons, the review which in union with you We have been able to make of the various problems of modern social life from the dawn of the teaching of Pope Leo XIII, has been, as it were, an unfolding of a series of statements and resolves on which We invite you to dwell, meditate deeply and to take courage in the co-operation of all for the realisation on earth of the kingdom of Christ : "a kingdom of truth and of life; a kingdom of holiness and grace; a kingdom of justice, of love and peace," that assures the enjoyment of the heavenly goods for which we were created and for which we long. Here one is concerned with the doctrine of the Catholic and Apostolic Church, Mother and Teacher of all the nations, whose light illumines, enkindles and inflames, whose warning voice filled with heavenly wisdom pertains to all times, whose power ever offers efficacious and suitable remedies for the increasing needs of men, for the deprivations and anxieties of the present life. That voice is in union with that of the Psalmist of old which unceasingly fortifies and lifts up our minds : "I will hear what the Lord will speak in me; for he will speak peace unto his people; and unto his saints; and unto them that are converted to the heart. Surely his salvation is near to them that fear him; that glory may dwell in our land. Mercy and truth have met each other; justice and peace have kissed. Truth is sprung out of the earth : and justice hath looked down from heaven. For the Lord will give goodness : and our earth shall yield her fruit. Justice shall walk before him : and shall set his steps in the way."

Such is the desire that We make in ending this Letter to which We have for a considerable time given Our solicitude for the universal Church. We desire that the Divine Redeemer of man, "who of God is made unto us wisdom and justice and sanctification and redemption," may reign and triumph gloriously throughout the ages, in all and over all; We desire that human society being restored to order, all nations may firmly enjoy prosperity, happiness and peace. As a portent of these wishes and as a pledge of Our paternal good will may the Apostolic Blessing, which We give from Our heart in the Lord, descend on you, venerable brethren and on all the faithful entrusted to your care and especially on those who will reply with generosity to Our appeals.